You Can Cook This!

You Can Cook This!

Turn the 30 Most Commonly Wasted Foods into 135 Delicious Plant-Based Meals

Max La Manna

RODALE

Introduction 7

In the Kitchen 9

1 Root Vegetables 15

Carrot
Parsnip
Potato
Beet

2 Grains 49

Rice
Mixed Grains
Pasta
Bread

3 Nightshades 83

Tomato
Eggplant
Pepper

4 Gourds & Legumes 111

Pumpkin
Squash
Cucumber
Tofu
Chickpeas
Beans

14 Quick Recipe Hacks   256
How to Get the Best Out of Your Food!   270
Occasion Index   276
Index   278
Notes   284
Acknowledgments   287

5 Leafy Greens & Cruciferous — 141

Cauliflower
Broccoli
Herbs

6 Fungi & Alliums — 173

Mushrooms
Onion
Garlic

7 Non-Dairy — 205

Milk
Yogurt

8 Fruits — 223

Apple
Banana
Berries
Citrus

9 Leftovers — 239

Introduction

If you ask me what I love the most, I would say to you without hesitation—food (really sorry to my wife; she knows this already, and she's a close second). I have never been shy to talk about food or my passion for wasting less of it.

First and foremost, my love of food means that I simply enjoy cooking and eating it, and I hate seeing it wasted. However, I grew up in the US, which is without a doubt one of the most wasteful countries in the world, and its throw-away food culture is no exception.

It's not just pre-packaged fast and cheap food that is treated as disposable: the same ethos is found in high-end restaurants, too. During my time trying to make it as an actor, I worked at an array of restaurants in Los Angeles and New York City, including one with a Michelin star. Food waste was rife at all of them. It pained me.

Once I admitted defeat against my acting aspirations, I turned my focus to championing the food we already have in our fridges and cupboards, and finding exciting new ways to cook the meals we crave the most. I did this in person by hosting dinners for friends, corporate events, and demonstrations, and then later on a digital scale, creating content that is accessible and easy to follow for as many people as possible.

The recipes I've created are here to inspire, excite, and transform the way you cook, store, and save food. You may be someone who cooks every day, or perhaps you're someone who wants to learn or cook more; whoever you are, whatever your motivation, this book is a practical guide, showing you how to develop and cook delicious, simple dishes with the food you already have in your kitchen.

You Can Cook This!—and you probably should! Get in the kitchen right now, explore your fridge and cupboards, uncover the neglected and forgotten ingredients—as long as it's safe to eat and there isn't mold growing on it—and cook your way through these pages. You'll see how effortless it is to create meals using what you already have, and what's more, they'll save you money and time.

Why I Wrote This Cookbook

Before we start cooking, I need to say a BIG thank-you to those of you who follow me on social media. I asked you for ideas and inspiration; you may recall the question boxes on my Instagram stories that said: "Tell me the food you waste the most," and from this simple question, I had tens of thousands of responses. Collecting the data, I've narrowed it down to the top 30 most-wasted ingredients in your homes. I don't think you're going to be surprised by the focus-led ingredients in this cookbook—you'll already be familiar with most of them. However, I think you may be encouraged by how easy it is to cook these recipes and waste less food.

How This Cookbook Works

It's easier than ever to cook mouth-watering dishes for yourself and your loved ones. This is how it works: all you need is to find an ingredient you want to cook, head to the chapter with said ingredient, and there you'll find delicious, easy-to-cook recipes to choose from. You'll find further inspiration in the Occasion Index (page 276). These recipes are designed to encourage you to use the entire vegetable, grain, or fruit so that there's no half-cut, rogue piece of onion or bagged salad wilting and rotting away in your fridge. In this book, there are classics with a twist like my Cauliflower Ragù (page 146); hearty meals such as Romesco Risotto (page 108); fan favorites like Tofu Butter "Chicken" (page 124) and Crispy Smashed Potatoes (page 36); indulgent sweet recipes, such as Salted Chocolate, Peanut Butter, and Tahini Brownies (page 219) and Carrot Pecan Cake and Orange Drizzle (page 46); comfort food, such as Beet Bucatini (page 30) or One-Pan Lasagna (page 84) and finger-licking snacks—don't miss my Spicy Baked Cauliflower Wings (page 148) and Loaded Nachos (page 19)!

There's a disproportionate amount of pressure placed on personal responsibility to create less waste in the world. The majority of this pressure should be redirected and placed on the world's top 100 most-polluting corporations—who are responsible for 71 percent of greenhouse gas emissions. Not all individuals have the privilege, time, and access to forgo plastic packaging and cook every meal from scratch. With that said, I have firsthand experience of how individual change—with the planet in mind—can benefit our mental health and sense of purpose and community. The more of us aboard this ship, the more positive change we can make.

Enjoy cooking, sharing, and eating delicious food.

— **Max**

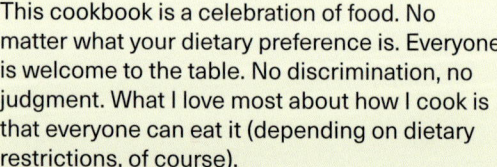

Everyone Is Welcome at the Table

This cookbook is a celebration of food. No matter what your dietary preference is. Everyone is welcome to the table. No discrimination, no judgment. What I love most about how I cook is that everyone can eat it (depending on dietary restrictions, of course).

Plant-based equivalents of butter and popular cheeses such as cheddar, feta, mozzarella, and parmesan have become easier to find in supermarkets, along with an array of non-dairy milks, yogurts, and creams. Feel free to experiment, or use dairy products if you prefer.

All of the recipes in this book have been tested with plant-based ingredients, as that's how I like to eat.

In the Kitchen

You have found yourself . . . in the kitchen. For me, the kitchen has always taken center stage. When I was growing up, it was the hub of our home and now, as an adult, it's where I spend most of my time. If I'm ever at a party, you can always find me in the kitchen. They say we sleep for one-third of our lives; I probably spend more than half my waking life in the kitchen (as I write this, I am in my kitchen).

The kitchen stores food and produces meals. It can be a well-oiled machine or it can be chaos. My kitchen is also my office, so I like to keep it in tip-top shape and clutter-free. What I'm talking about here is how you store your food. Quite simply, it can make or break your meals, and your bank account.

I'm often asked on social media and in person what easy steps we can all take to waste less food. Here are some actions to take to waste a little less food at home:

Make a list before shopping

Do a quick inventory of your fridge and cupboard and see which foods you already have on hand.

Cook

I know it seems obvious, but 40 percent of food waste is coming from unused produce in the home. Cook the food you already have, find a recipe (perhaps in this book), and start cooking.

Save your leftovers

Keep them in a sealed container either in your fridge or freezer and eat them the next day or later in the week.

Store food properly (see page 10 and 271)

Use technology and donate food; there are apps and charities where you can donate food or pick up food from others in your community.

Compost

Food doesn't belong in landfills. Did you know it takes 25 years for a head of lettuce to decompose in a landfill? Whereas if composted properly it would take 30–90 days and provide rich nutrients to the soil. Which of these sounds better to you? If you don't already have a food waste collection, either build a compost heap at home or contact your local government and find out about food waste recycling.

How to Store Food

When you think of storing food, what comes to mind? Do you imagine wrapping your dinner leftovers, putting them in the fridge, and calling it a day? All food can be classified under three groups: perishable, semi-perishable, and staple.

Perishable foods

This includes many raw fruits and vegetables—and for those who eat them, meat, dairy, and eggs. To store these foods for any length of time, they need to be held at the correct temperature. As a rule, the interior temperature of a fridge can vary between 35 and 40°F, but check with your health department for more accurate advice.

Semi-perishable foods

Flour, grains, dried fruits and seeds, nuts, and peanut butter are considered semi-perishable. If optimally stored, in a clean and airtight container kept in a cool, dry place, semi-perishable foods may remain unspoiled for a long time. Freeze them and they can last even longer.

Staple foods

Dried beans, pasta, rice, spices, and canned goods are all non-perishable foods. However, if they are stored incorrectly, they will spoil and lose their quality. Keep these ingredients in cool, dry conditions and out of sunlight. I keep my dried beans, pasta, and rice in airtight containers, my spices in sealed jars, and my canned goods in a cupboard out of direct sunlight.

The Fridge

The most common way many of us store produce is in the fridge. Always keep an eye on the temperature of your fridge and avoid overcrowding it. Stuffing your fridge with food can impact the air circulation inside, meaning that food can spoil even more rapidly. Every two weeks, take five minutes to go through your fridge and see what belongs and what doesn't. I like doing this because sometimes—even for me—food gets shoved to the back and is lost forever. For a more detailed overview of how to get the most out of your food through proper storage, I've included a table at the back of the book (page 271) that covers all the key ingredients used in this book.

- Fruits with stones, such as peaches and plums, should be placed in a closed paper bag until ripe, then kept in the fridge.

- Keep tomatoes at room temperature only if they'll be eaten within 1–2 days; otherwise, they go in the fridge. They like their space, so don't overcrowd them, and place them stem side down.

The Freezer

Along with pre-frozen foods, freeze leftovers, bread, and herbs. Before freezing, wrap and label food.

The Pantry/Kitchen Cupboards

These should be cool, dry, and, ideally, dark, to provide optimal storage conditions for pasta, rice and other grains, dried beans and lentils, flour, sugar, dried fruits, nuts and seeds, peanut butter, and canned goods.

- Keep potatoes in a cool, dark place.

- Onions and garlic also like a cool, dark place, but not in the same space as the potatoes. Store them separately.

1. **Top shelf**
   Leftovers to be consumed in 2–3 days, and use-by-date foods

2. **Middle shelf**
   Deli products

3. **Bottom shelf**
   Plant-based milk and yogurt

4. **Drawers**
   Fruits and vegetables

5. **Bottom door**
   Juice, condiments

6. **Top door**
   Plant-based butter and cheese

How to Clean Vegetables and Fruits

- Always wash produce before preparing; it's usually best to do this just before you use it.

- Remove and compost the outer leaves of leafy greens, such as cabbage and lettuce, if they seem like they've had better days.

- Wash your hands with warm, soapy water, then gently rub produce under running water. Use a vegetable brush on firmer produce.

- If you're worried about dirt or bugs, soak produce for a few minutes in a mix of 10 parts water to 1 part white vinegar. Salt can also be added to the mix.

Using Leftovers

Or what I like to call Tomorrow's Lunch. Please try not to throw away your leftovers. They often taste even better the next day!

- Cool leftovers as quickly as possible once they've been cooked, ideally within two hours.

- Divide leftovers into portions, then chill or freeze.

- If chilling, use within three days.

- Always defrost leftovers completely, either in the fridge or on the worktop.

- When defrosted, reheat only once. The more times you cool and reheat food, the higher the risk of food poisoning.

- When reheating food, ensure it reaches 160°F for two minutes to kill off any bacteria.

- For safety and to waste less food, only take out of the freezer what you intend to consume within 24 hours.

Food Labeling: What Does It All Mean?

I have a confession: I was confused by this a few years ago, but once I wrapped my head around it, I finally conquered this confusing labeling system. It's one area that is often overlooked when preventing food waste.

Best-before/Use-by

Best-before and use-by dates are all about the quality. Enjoy this food before or on this date. After this date, it is safe to eat, but may not be at its best. Use your best judgment. Inspect it, smell it, taste a tiny amount of it.

Sell-by

Sell-by dates are to inform the shop to sell this product. This is for the shop only and you can most certainly ignore this, but use your judgment before buying. I like buying sell-by-date bread when I see it and freezing it as soon as I get home. It's usually on sale, too!

Chop Chop: Simple Preparation to Waste Less Food

In every food preparation, there is some element of "waste," right? What if I told you I can help you minimize the amount of food that's tossed away?

At the back of this book (page 270) you will find a simple guide that will show you how to get ahead and waste less by properly prepping all of the key ingredients used in this book. By introducing these small hacks into your food preparation you will reduce food waste, save money, and send less to landfills. Prepping ingredients before you start to cook can also save time: you won't need to stop mid-recipe to chop herbs or zest a lemon. Remember:

- Eat the skin. Don't peel potatoes, carrots, apples, pears, and kiwis.
- Perk up your water. Add peelings from citrus fruits or cucumber to a jug of cold water.
- Be a seed saver. Bake, toast, or fry the seeds from butternut squash and pumpkin.
- Pulse your bread in a food processor. Freeze breadcrumbs to use in stuffings and toppings.
- Blend it up.
- Add leafy greens to smoothies; blend and freeze herbs, garlic, and ginger in ice cube trays.
- Make a veg stock with scraps (page 260).
- Save leftovers to eat tomorrow.
- Keep your fridge clutter-free.
- Use your freezer more often.
- Compost, if you can.
- Don't worry about being perfect.

How to Use This Book

Following the recipes you will often find tips and tricks to help you get the best results and avoid waste. You will also see the following icons:

Serves/Makes	Gives you an idea of how many the dish will feed. That may depend on your appetite, and whether you serve it as a main or side dish.	**Leftovers**	Tells you how long leftovers will keep, covered or wrapped, in the fridge.
Prep Time	This includes chopping but not marinating, chilling, or rising times for dough.	**Freezer Friendly**	Tells you how long you can keep leftovers in the freezer.
Cook Time	The amount of time in the oven or on the stove. This may vary depending on the size of the ingredient.	**Gluten Free** **GF**	Tells you that the recipe is entirely gluten free. I have included separate tips on how to make simple swaps if you need a gluten-free option.

1– Root Vegetables

Carrot
Parsnip
Potato
Beet

Carrot Lox and Bagel

If you go for a walk in Brooklyn on a Sunday, I'd guess that one in every ten people will have a bagel with smoked salmon and cream cheese in their hands! I teased this recipe on social media and EVERYONE wanted to know how to make it. It's the first time I'm sharing it—and I promise you won't be disappointed! Surprisingly easy to make, carrot strips soften in the marinade, becoming deliciously chewy. It is the perfect balance of smoky spices, mimicking the texture and taste of smoked salmon. Pile it high on a bagel with cream cheese, Pickled Red Onion, and capers. What more can you ask for?

4 large carrots
3 Tbsp olive oil
1 Tbsp rice vinegar
2 tsp liquid smoke
½ tsp smoked paprika
¼ tsp black pepper
pinch of salt

To serve
4 bagels or slices of toast
5¼–7 oz cream cheese (see note)
Pickled Red Onion (page 267)
capers
finely chopped chives

1 Preheat the oven to 300°F. Line a baking sheet with parchment paper.

2 Using a vegetable peeler, peel the carrots into long, thin ribbons. Place the ribbons on the baking sheet and bake for 10–12 minutes, until soft. Remove from the oven and set aside to cool.

3 Meanwhile, in a bowl or container, whisk together the remaining ingredients.

4 Add the carrots to the marinade and gently massage to combine. Cover and keep in the fridge for at least 1 hour or overnight.

5 Serve on a bagel or toast, spread with a layer of cream cheese. Top with carrot lox, pickled red onion, and capers, then sprinkle with chopped chives.

> **Note** If a recipe calls for a dairy product, please know that you can use your favorite plant-based equivalent. All of the recipes in this book have been tested with plant-based ingredients, as that's how I like to eat.

Tip Remember to allow least 1 hour for the carrot to marinate.

 4   15 mins   10–12 mins   Up to 7 days

Roasted Parsnip and Celeriac with Garlicky Grains and Creamy Tahini Sauce

Served on a big platter in the middle of the table, hearty root vegetables bring comfort to dark winter days. Roasting the veg enhances their sweet, earthy flavors, with cumin and a subtle bittersweet sharpness and licorice taste from the caraway seeds. Served on garlicky grains, it's all brought together by a creamy tahini sauce.

2 lb combination of parsnips
  and celeriac
4 Tbsp olive oil
1 tsp ground cumin
1 tsp caraway seeds
1 head of garlic
1¼ cups barley, freekeh, or brown rice
2 small bunches of fresh herbs
  (I used parsley and tarragon)
zest and juice of 2 lemons
2 Tbsp tahini
1 tsp whole-grain mustard
pinch of sugar (optional)
salt and black pepper
sesame seeds, to garnish

1 Heat the oven to 400°F.

2 Slice the parsnips in half lengthwise and the celeriac into roughly 1¼–½-inch chunks. Place them in a roasting pan and toss with 2 tablespoons of the olive oil, the cumin, and the caraway seeds. Snuggle the whole garlic into the pan and roast for 35–40 minutes.

3 Meanwhile, cook your grains according to the package instructions, then drain and tip into a bowl. Roughly chop the herbs and add most to the bowl, reserving some for a garnish. Add the zest and juice of 1 lemon, along with the remaining olive oil. Season with salt and pepper and toss well.

4 Mix the tahini with the mustard and the zest and juice of half a lemon. Adding 1 tablespoon of water at a time, mix until it has a drizzleable consistency. Season well with salt and pepper. Taste and add a pinch of sugar if it feels a little sharp.

5 Once the veg is cooked, take the garlic and squeeze it into the grains; it should be soft and golden. Mix well, then tip the garlicky grains onto a platter. Top with the roasted parsnips and celeriac. Drizzle with the zesty tahini sauce, scatter with the sesame seeds and remaining herbs, and serve with the zest and juice of the remaining half lemon.

Tip Play around with different veg, such as fennel, carrot, sweet potato, rutabaga, and beet.

 4–8
 10 mins
 35–40 mins
 Up to 7 days
 Up to 1 month

Loaded Nachos and Carrot Cheese Sauce

Nachos are the ideal party dish to bring everyone to the table. You can swap in chickpeas or kidney beans and play around with the other toppings, but the hero of the dish is the creamy, cheesy, velvety sauce. It's great poured over roasted cauliflower or baked potatoes, too.

1–2 large packs of tortilla chips
1 (14-oz) can black beans, drained
  and rinsed
¼ red cabbage, thinly shredded
½ recipe Killer Tofu "Ground Beef"
  (page 128)

Carrot nacho cheese
2 medium carrots, not peeled and
  roughly chopped
4 small new potatoes, not peeled and
  roughly chopped
2 garlic cloves
1 Tbsp tomato purée
2 tsp cornstarch
¼ cup milk (I use oat)
juice of ½ lemon
3 Tbsp nutritional yeast
1 tsp chili powder
½ tsp ground turmeric
pinch of salt
¼ tsp black pepper

Sour cream
¾ cup raw cashews, soaked in hot
  water for 20–30 minutes, or overnight
2 Tbsp apple cider vinegar
juice of ½ lemon
½ cup cold water
pinch of salt

To serve (your choice)
halved cherry tomatoes, shredded
  lettuce, sliced red chiles, Pickled
  Red Onion (page 267), black olives,
  roughly chopped fresh cilantro, lime
  wedges, guacamole, salsa

1 To make the carrot nacho cheese: bring a pan of salted water to a boil, add the carrots and potatoes, and cook for about 10 minutes, until soft. Drain well, then transfer the veg to a high-speed blender. Add all the remaining ingredients and blend until very smooth. Set aside.

2 To make the vegan sour cream: drain the soaked cashews and rinse in cold water. Add all the remaining ingredients to a high-speed blender and blend until very smooth. Set aside.

3 Preheat the oven to 350°F.

4 In a large baking pan, add a layer of tortilla chips, black beans, red cabbage, and a drizzle of the nacho cheese. Add a second layer of tortilla chips with my killer tofu "ground beef" and another drizzle of nacho cheese, then bake for 8–10 minutes, until lightly crispy and golden brown.

5 Remove the nachos from the oven and top with the sour cream, plus your choice of cherry tomatoes, shredded lettuce, sliced chiles, pickled red onion, black olives, and fresh cilantro. Serve hot, with lime wedges to squeeze over, and guacamole and salsa on the side.

Tips Most tortilla chips are made from corn, which is naturally gluten free, but if gluten is an issue for you, check the label.

When making the Killer Tofu "Ground Beef," use tamari, a version of soy sauce made without wheat.

The nachos will serve 2 as a main meal or 6 as a side or sharing dish.

If you want to make the vegan sour cream, put the cashews to soak before you start to cook—or even the night before.

The carrot nacho cheese will keep in the fridge for 3–5 days, or in the freezer for 1 month.

 2–6   10 mins   20 mins **GF**

Creamy Leek and Parsnip Soup with Parsnip Peel Chips

Leeks and parsnips go hand in hand in this sweet and earthy soup, with a flash of fire from ginger and turmeric, lifted by fresh lemon and finished with Carrot Top Pesto. Bringing all the drama and impact to your table, a tower of baked parsnip chips transforms a simple bowl of soup into something spectacular!

6 parsnips, 5 not peeled and cut into ½-inch pieces, reserve 1 for garnish
2 Tbsp extra-virgin olive oil
2 large leeks, including tops, cut into ½-inch pieces
1½ tsp salt
1 tsp black pepper
1 bay leaf
1 tsp ground turmeric
4 garlic cloves, minced
1 Tbsp grated fresh ginger
1 shallot, diced
4 cups veg stock or water
zest and juice of 1 lemon

To serve
4 tsp olive oil
4 Tbsp crème fraîche (see note on page 16)
4 Tbsp Carrot Top Pesto (page 28)

1 Preheat the oven to 350°F.

2 With a vegetable peeler, peel 1 parsnip into long, thin ribbons. Place the peelings on a lined baking sheet and bake in the oven for about 7 minutes, until crispy and golden; keep an eye on them so they don't burn. Set aside while you make the soup.

3 Heat the oil in a large saucepan or Dutch oven over medium heat. Add the leeks, 5 remaining parsnips, salt, and black pepper, and cook, stirring occasionally, for 8–10 minutes.

4 Add the bay leaf, turmeric, garlic, ginger, and shallot, and cook for 3–5 minutes until the veg is soft and fragrant. Increase the heat to high, pour in the stock, and bring to a boil. Reduce the heat and simmer for 8–10 minutes.

5 Remove the bay leaf, then use an immersion blender to purée the veg with the lemon zest and juice until it has a creamy consistency. If you like a thinner consistency, add a little extra stock or water and purée again.

6 Remove from the heat and serve the soup with the parsnip peel chips, a drizzle of olive oil, the crème fraîche, and carrot top pesto.

 4   10 mins   30–35 mins   Up to 3 days   Up to 1 month   GF

Midweek Carrot and Potato Bake

Weeknight cooking doesn't get much easier than a sheet-pan recipe. You place everything in a sheet pan and then let the oven do the job for you! This colorful dish is great served in the middle of the table if you have friends over, too. Don't skip the herby yogurt sauce: it's bright, fresh, and cooling, balancing the earthy, smoky, spicy flavors of the veg.

1⅓ lb carrots, not peeled
2 lb potatoes, not peeled (I use a mix of
    sweet potatoes and new potatoes)
2 red onions, cut into chunky wedges
1 garlic head
2 Tbsp olive oil
12 oz plant-based sausages
6–8 Tbsp tagine paste
handful of fresh parsley, roughly
    chopped
⅓ cup almonds, toasted and roughly
    chopped
salt and black pepper

Minty yogurt
zest and juice of 1 lime
3 Tbsp chopped fresh mint leaves
½ cup yogurt (see note on page 16)
pinch of salt

1   Preheat the oven to 400°F.

2   Give the carrots a quick wash and slice into 3-inch pieces. Roughly chop the potatoes into wedges and quarter the new potatoes; the key is to keep the veg at similar sizes so they cook evenly.

3   Arrange in a large sheet pan along with the onion wedges. Snuggle in the garlic, drizzle with olive oil, season with salt and black pepper, and roast for 15–20 minutes.

4   Add the sausages to the pan, along with the tagine paste, toss well, and roast for 15–20 minutes, until the carrots and potatoes are crisp and the sausages are browned.

5   Meanwhile, in a food processor or blender, blend the minty yogurt ingredients until smooth and vibrant.

6   Squeeze the flesh from the garlic into the tray and give everything a final toss. Drizzle with most of the minty yogurt and finish with the parsley and toasted almonds. Serve straight from the pan, with the remaining minty yogurt for people to add at the table.

Tips   Try it with different spice pastes—any kind of curry paste or even Thai green curry. Or get creative and make your own!

Try subbing celeriac for the carrots.

If storing leftovers in the freezer, be sure to allow them to come to room temperature before heating up in the oven.

 4–8   15 mins   30–40 mins   Up to 7 days   Up to 1 month   **GF**

Carrots and Beets with Tahini Balsamic Vinaigrette

This colorful salad goes with everything from burgers or slow-roasted veg to my Nut Roast Cake with All the Trimmings (page 70), Grilled Zucchini and Miso-Almond "Ricotta" Involtini (page 121), or Zesty and Herby Summer Orzo Salad (page 52). Stunning as a side dish on a festive table or perfect for a midweek lunch.

⅓ cup shelled pistachios
2 Tbsp extra-virgin olive oil
2 tsp balsamic vinegar
1 Tbsp tahini
zest and juice of 1 lemon
1 tsp Dijon mustard
5 carrots, peeled lengthwise into ribbons
3 small beets (any color), peeled and thinly sliced on a mandoline
2 Tbsp chopped fresh mint
salt and black pepper

1 In a small frying pan over medium heat, toast the pistachios until lightly brown, shaking the pan occasionally; this should take 3–5 minutes. Leave to cool and then chop roughly. Set aside.

2 Whisk together the olive oil, balsamic vinegar, tahini, lemon juice, and mustard until smooth and creamy. Set aside.

3 Place the carrots and beets in a large bowl. Pour over half the dressing and toss to coat; season to taste with salt and pepper. Leave for 6–8 minutes so the beets soften up a little bit.

4 Transfer the carrots and beets to a large serving plate or bowl and spoon over the rest of the dressing. Scatter over the lemon zest, chopped mint, and pistachios.

Tip Want more bulk? Add crumbled feta.

 4–8   15 mins   5 mins Up to 3 days

Carrot Top Pesto

I have to be honest: I used to throw away my carrot tops all the time, mainly because I didn't know what to do with them, and they took up too much space in the fridge. I've since turned over a new leaf. Make sure that you wash the tops thoroughly to remove any earth. You'll be left with a beautiful green bouquet that makes a deliciously earthy pesto. This fan favorite is great for pasta and pizzas.

green tops from a large bunch of carrots, rinsed and bottoms trimmed
1 bunch of fresh basil, including stems
3 Tbsp sunflower or pumpkin seeds
3 Tbsp raw cashews or almonds
2 garlic cloves
5 Tbsp nutritional yeast
2 Tbsp cold water
5 Tbsp extra-virgin olive oil

1 Put the carrot tops, basil, seeds, nuts, garlic, nutritional yeast, and water into a food processor.

2 Begin to blend at a low speed, then slowly stream in the olive oil as you increase the speed, until mostly smooth.

Tip Pesto can be made 1 day ahead. Store in a clean jar or container, and pour in a ¼-inch layer of olive oil to prevent browning. Keep in the fridge.

 8 +   5 mins   Up to 2 weeks   Up to 1 month   GF

Quick Pickled Carrots

Ready in minutes, these super-speedy pickled carrots add instant crunch, acidity, and an amazing flash of color to brighten any dish. Try them on rice dishes, in stir-fries, on top of the Loaded Nachos on page 19, in a crispy tofu sandwich, or in the tacos on page 142.

1 lb carrots, sliced diagonally, ¼ inch thick, or grated
1 Tbsp black peppercorns
1 Tbsp black or brown mustard seeds
1 tsp coriander seeds
¾ cup white wine vinegar or apple cider vinegar
3 Tbsp water
3 Tbsp sugar
2 tsp salt

1 Put the carrots into a large sterilized canning jar. Add the peppercorns, mustard seeds, and coriander seeds and set aside.

2 Put the vinegar, water, sugar, and salt in a pan over medium heat and simmer, stirring, until the sugar and salt are fully dissolved.

3 Pour the warm brine over the carrots, ensuring that the carrots are fully submerged. If needed, add more vinegar or water to cover them.

4 Securely seal the jar, then shake to combine. Chill for at least 30 minutes to 1 hour before serving. For optimal flavor, marinate overnight or for up to 24 hours.

Tips For a spicier flavor, add 1 tsp red pepper flakes and 2 garlic cloves, thinly sliced or crushed.

Keep in a sealed jar in the fridge for up to 2 weeks.

You can sub the carrots for beets. They will have an incredible color!

 8 +   15 mins   10 mins   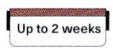 Up to 2 weeks   **GF**

Beet Bucatini

Be amazed at how the beet turns the pasta a majestic ruby red in this creamy, vibrant dish. It's enough to convince anyone that beets are incredible. Add the sauce to anything from salads to pizza to pasta. This is one of my favorite dishes in this book!

12 oz bucatini, spaghetti, or linguine
¼ cup crumbled feta, to serve (see note on page 16)

Beet sauce
1 large beet
1 Tbsp olive oil
1 onion, chopped
2 garlic cloves, finely chopped or crushed
1 Tbsp chopped parsley stems
1 Tbsp chopped fresh basil stems, plus basil leaves to garnish
4 Tbsp nutritional yeast
juice of ½ lemon
1 tsp salt
½ tsp black pepper
5 Tbsp oat milk, or more as needed

Crispy garlic breadcrumbs
1 Tbsp olive oil
1 garlic clove, grated or thinly sliced
⅔ cup breadcrumbs (homemade from a stale loaf, or store-bought)

Tips Use gluten-free pasta and breadcrumbs if you prefer.

Store any leftover pasta and garlic breadcrumbs separately.

1 To make the beet sauce: bring a pan of water to a boil, add the beet, and cook for 10–15 minutes or until tender. Drain and set aside to cool for a few minutes, then trim, slip off peel, and cut into quarters.

2 Meanwhile, in a non-stick frying pan over medium heat, heat the olive oil and cook the onion, garlic, and parsley and basil stems for 3–5 minutes, until fragrant and soft. Remove from the heat; do not wash the pan.

3 Put the beet into a food processor or blender, add the onion mixture, nutritional yeast, lemon juice, salt, and pepper. Pulse for 1 minute, then, with the motor still running, stream in the oat milk. Blend on high speed until very smooth. If the sauce is too thick, add a little more milk, 1 tablespoon at a time, to loosen.

4 Bring a large pan of salted water to a boil, add the bucatini, and cook for 9 minutes or until al dente. Drain the pasta, reserving 4–5 tablespoons of the pasta cooking water.

5 Meanwhile, prepare the crispy garlic breadcrumbs. In a separate frying pan, heat the oil over medium heat, add the garlic, and fry for 1 minute until lightly browned. Add the breadcrumbs and cook, stirring frequently, until the breadcrumbs are lightly charred and fragrant, 2–3 minutes. Remove from the heat and set aside.

6 In the same frying pan used for the onion and garlic, add the cooked pasta and beet sauce and stir well over low–medium heat for 2 minutes. If too thick, stir in some of the reserved pasta water.

7 Serve the pasta in bowls or on plates, garnished with roughly torn basil leaves, crumbled feta cheese, and crispy garlic breadcrumbs.

 4 15 mins 25–35 mins 1–2 days Up to 1 month

Marinated Beets with Toasted Pistachios, Orange, and Mint

Baked until tender, the beets are then marinated with shallot and ginger. Orange segments, cinnamon, toasted pistachios, and fresh mint are added just before serving on creamy yogurt to make a complex, sweet autumnal salad.

4 yellow or red beets
½ cup sherry vinegar or rice vinegar
4 Tbsp olive oil
¼ cup water
1 shallot, finely chopped
1 Tbsp grated fresh ginger
1 orange, zested, then segmented
¼ tsp ground cinnamon
¼ cup raw pistachios, toasted and chopped
2 Tbsp chopped fresh mint
1 cup thick yogurt (or oat or coconut)
salt and black pepper

1   Preheat the oven to 400°F.

2   Put the beets in a baking dish. In a small bowl, mix ¼ cup of the vinegar, 2 tablespoons of the olive oil, the water, and salt and pepper. Pour over the beets and toss until well coated. Cover with foil and bake for about 40 minutes, until soft and tender. Remove from the oven and leave to cool for 5–10 minutes, then trim, slip off the peels, and cut into quarters while still warm.

3   Meanwhile, in a large bowl, mix the shallot and ginger with the remaining vinegar and olive oil, and season with a pinch of salt. Add the warm beet quarters, toss to coat, and leave in the fridge to marinate for at least 45 minutes and up to 3 days.

4   To serve, add the orange segments, cinnamon, and most of the pistachios and mint to the beets and gently combine.

5   Spread the yogurt over the base of a serving plate, top with the marinated beets, and sprinkle over the orange zest and the remaining pistachios and mint.

Tips Marinate the beets up to 2–3 days ahead, cover, and chill.

If you buy beets with their green tops, you can chop the greens and cook them like spinach, or use the greens instead of carrot tops in the Carrot Top Pesto on page 28.

 6   15 mins   40 mins   Up to 3 days   **GF**

The Best Roasted Potatoes

Since living in the UK, I've realized I've been cooking roasted potatoes wrong my entire life! As all Brits know, the secret is to boil the potatoes for a few minutes first, then rough up the outsides before cooking them in the oven in already-hot oil. This three-stage process will guarantee you perfect roasties every time!

4 lb large potatoes, not peeled, cut into 2-inch pieces
7 Tbsp olive oil
2 Tbsp vegetable oil
2 Tbsp butter (see note on page 16)
6 garlic cloves, crushed
4 long fresh rosemary sprigs
6 fresh thyme sprigs
salt

1   Preheat the oven to 425°F.

2   Put the potatoes in a large pan of salted water. Bring to a boil over medium-high heat, then reduce to a simmer and cook for about 5 minutes, until the potatoes are fork-tender on the outside but still firm in the middle.

3   When the potatoes are nearly ready, add the oils and butter to a large roasting pan, stir together, then place in the hot oven for at least 5 minutes until the oils and butter are hot.

4   Drain the potatoes well, then return them to their pan, uncovered, to steam-dry for about 2 minutes. Holding the lid on securely with both hands, give the pan a good shake, just enough to fluff up the outer edges of the potatoes; don't shake the pan too hard or the potatoes will break apart.

5   Take the roasting pan out of the oven and carefully coat the potatoes in the hot oils. Spread out the potatoes to keep them separate in the roasting pan as this will ensure each one gets super-crispy in the oven. Roast the potatoes for 20 minutes, turning them halfway through. If they are browning too quickly, reduce the heat.

6   Add the garlic, rosemary, and thyme sprigs, turn the potatoes again, then return to the oven for a further 10 minutes, until the potatoes are golden brown and the skin is deliciously crispy. Transfer the potatoes, garlic, thyme, and rosemary to a serving plate using a slotted spoon or tongs to drain off any excess oil.

Tip These roasties are great as a side dish with my Roast Dinner Tart (page 119) and Nut Roast Cake on page 70.

 8   5 mins   35–40 mins   Up to 7 days   **GF**

Potato and Spring Onion Cakes

If you have some potatoes languishing in a drawer, use them in these potato cakes today! Just pull off any shoots, but if the potatoes have turned green, it's best to compost them. With the crunchy Asian-style slaw, this is a great brunch or light lunch, or make mini versions to serve as canapés.

2 lb potatoes
splash of milk (see note on page 16)
2 Tbsp self-rising flour, plus more for dusting
2 tsp grated fresh ginger
1 bunch spring onions, finely sliced
½ small bunch of fresh cilantro, roughly chopped
3 Tbsp olive oil
salt and black pepper
coconut yogurt, to serve

Hispi slaw
1 hispi cabbage, shredded
½ small bunch of fresh cilantro, roughly chopped, plus more to garnish
2 Tbsp sesame seeds
zest and juice of 2 limes
1 Tbsp sesame oil
1 tsp sugar

1   Cut the potatoes into large chunks, cover with cold salted water in a large plan, placed over high heat, and bring to a boil. Cook for about 15 minutes, until very soft. Drain well in a colander and allow to steam-dry for 3–5 minutes.

2   Meanwhile, mix all ingredients for the slaw together in a large bowl, season with a generous pinch of salt, and set aside.

3   Mash the potatoes and milk in a large bowl; it's fine if there are a few chunks of potatoes. Season with salt and pepper. Add the flour, ginger, spring onions, and cilantro and set aside. Preheat the oven to 250°F.

4   Roll the potato mixture into 12 even balls, then dust with flour. Heat the olive oil in a large frying pan. Add the mashed potato balls, 4 at a time, and using the back of a spatula, press down to flatten them. Fry for 5–7 minutes on each side until golden brown and crispy.

5   Set the cakes aside on a lined baking sheet and slide into the oven to keep warm while you cook the rest. Keep an eye on the cooked cakes so they don't overcook and dry out; reduce the heat if needed.

6   Serve the potato cakes garnished with cilantro leaves and topped with a dollop of the yogurt, with the slaw on the side.

Tips If you have leftover mashed potatoes, give them new life in these potato cakes.

You can use any potatoes—sweet potatoes are great, or even celeriac.

 12 cakes   10 mins   1 hour   Up to 3 days   Up to 1 month

Crispy Smashed Potatoes with Spicy Lemon Mayo

This is a BIG fan favorite. Brushing the potatoes with tomato purée before roasting them gives them an amazing rich color and a surprise extra layer of flavor. I love to serve these as part of a savory brunch, with scrambled tofu, baked mushrooms, and roasted tomatoes. But they also make a fantastic starter or side dish.

20 new potatoes, not peeled
1 Tbsp extra-virgin olive oil
1 Tbsp tomato purée
zest and juice of ½ lemon
generous pinch of salt
¼ tsp black pepper
4 Tbsp mayonnaise
1 tsp smoked paprika
¼ tsp chili powder

To serve
Pickled Red Onion (page 267)
2 Tbsp roughly chopped fresh dill
2 Tbsp roughly chopped fresh chives

1   Preheat the oven to 400°F.

2   Bring a large pan of salted water to a boil, add the potatoes, and cook for 10–15 minutes, until they are just soft enough that you can poke a fork into them, then drain.

3   Meanwhile, whisk the olive oil, tomato purée, lemon zest, salt, and pepper until smooth.

4   Gently press the potatoes with the base of an empty jam jar until the skins break, then place them on a large baking sheet. Brush each potato with the oil and tomato mixture and bake for 20 minutes or until golden and the edges are crispy, rotating the baking sheet after about 10 minutes.

5   To a small bowl or jar, add the mayo, smoked paprika, chili powder, and lemon juice and stir or shake for a few seconds until smooth and combined.

6   Put the crispy potatoes on a serving platter and top with a few dollops of the spicy lemon mayo, some pickled red onion, and fresh herbs.

Tips Smaller potatoes are best.

For a main meal you may like to add some grated cheese after baking or serve with some steamed peas.

If you have any leftover potatoes*, keep them in the fridge and reheat until crispy.

 2–4   15 mins   30–35 mins   1–2 days*   Up to 3 months (Just potatoes)

Soft and Fluffy Potato Rolls

Whether you're cooking these rolls from scratch or using leftover mashed or baked potatoes, you're in luck: they're better than any rolls you can buy! You don't need to be an expert baker to make these gorgeous fluffy rolls as the dough is very forgiving, even if you over- or under-knead it. As with any yeast dough, you'll need to allow 1½–2 hours for the dough to rise—but you're free to get on with other things in that time. These fan favorites have a buttery, salty top and a super-soft center—perfect for sandwiches, or use them for my Super "Meatball" Sliders (page 68).

1¼ cups warm water
2¼ tsp active dry yeast
1 tsp sugar
4¾ cups all-purpose flour or gluten-free flour, plus more for dusting
2 tsp salt
6½ Tbsp butter, at room temperature (see note on page 16)
1¼ cups mashed potatoes (skins on)
vegetable oil, for greasing
flaky sea salt, for sprinkling

1 In a small bowl, whisk together the warm water, yeast, and sugar for about 1 minute, until the sugar has dissolved and the mixture is foamy. Set aside for about 5 minutes.

2 Mix the flour and salt in a large bowl, then add the yeast mixture, 4 Tbsp of the butter, and the mashed potatoes. Using your hands or a mixer fitted with a dough hook, knead well until all the ingredients are incorporated and the dough begins to feel smooth. Shape into a ball, drizzle a little oil around the inside of the bowl so the dough doesn't stick to it, cover with a clean kitchen towel, and leave for about 1 hour, or until doubled in size.

3 Grease a 9 x 13-inch baking pan with oil. Dust the worktop with flour. Punch the dough to deflate, then tip it onto the worktop and divide and roll into 12 equal balls. Place the balls in the greased baking pan and leave to proof for 30–45 minutes.

4 Preheat the oven to 400°F.

5 Melt the remaining butter and brush it over the top of each dough ball. Sprinkle with flaky sea salt and bake for 25 minutes, until the tops are golden brown and the rolls are baked through. Test by tapping the underside of a roll: it should sound hollow. Transfer to a wire rack to cool slightly before serving.

Tips If you prefer, use gluten-free flour.

Swap in sweet potato for the white.

Mash the potatoes until smooth or leave a few lumps—it's your call.

Keep leftovers, but not in the fridge, for up to 5 days.

 12 rolls 20 mins 25 mins Up to 1 month

Spiced Potato Pancakes

This recipe is inspired by dosas: thin pancakes originating in South India, made from a fermented batter and curled into a dome and often filled with spicy potatoes. I was motivated to make this recipe because potatoes are one of the most-wasted foods around the world. In the UK alone, over 4 million of them are wasted every day—that could make a lot of pancakes! The recipe is super-quick and easy to make, although making the pancakes requires a bit of practice. Follow along here, then fill your pancakes with spiced potatoes and serve with an Indian chutney.

Spiced potatoes
10 oz baby potatoes, not peeled, cut
  in half
2 Tbsp butter (see note on page 16)
2 Tbsp milk
2 Tbsp olive oil
1 onion, finely chopped
1 Tbsp grated fresh ginger
1 tsp black mustard seeds
1 tsp coriander seeds
2 tsp garam masala
½ tsp ground turmeric
4 curry leaves
3½ oz spinach or chopped kale
salt and black pepper

Pancakes
⅔ cup chickpea flour
⅔ cup buckwheat flour
1½ tsp baking soda
pinch of salt

To serve
chutney of your choice
  (I've served them with mango
  chutney)
Greek yogurt

1   Bring a pan of salted water to a boil, add the potatoes, and cook for 10–15 minutes, until soft. Drain off all the water and let the potatoes sit in the pan, uncovered, for a few minutes. In a bowl, lightly mash the potatoes with the butter and the milk until slightly chunky; season with salt and pepper. Set aside.

2   In a large frying pan, heat the oil over medium heat and fry the onion and ginger for 7–8 minutes, until soft and fragrant. Add the mustard seeds and coriander seeds and let them cook for a few minutes until they pop, then add the garam masala, turmeric, and curry leaves and cook, stirring, for 1 minute.

3   Lower the heat and add the mashed potatoes to the onion mixture, then stir in the spinach or kale until wilted. Splash in a little water if the potatoes stick to the pan. Set aside.

4   To make the pancakes, mix all the ingredients in a bowl, adding enough water to make a pourable, runny batter. Heat a non-stick flat griddle or a large non-stick frying pan over medium-high heat. Pour about half a ladleful of the batter onto the center of the griddle, then quickly and confidently spread the batter around the griddle, using the bottom of the ladle in a circular motion. The pancake should be fairly thin, and dry on the top. Cook, without flipping, for 1–2 minutes, until golden brown and the edges are crispy and beginning to curl. Remove from the griddle and cook 3 more pancakes in the same way.

5   Serve the spiced potatoes with the pancakes, chutney, and yogurt.

 4   10 mins   25–35 mins   1–3 days*   Up to 1 month   **GF**

Tips *Keep spiced potatoes in the fridge for 1–3 days. You can make them in advance, but make the pancakes just before you are ready to eat.

Chickpea flour is gluten-free. Buckwheat flour is naturally gluten-free, but brands vary; if gluten is an issue for you, check the label.

Roasted Sweet Potatoes with Creamy and Zesty Tahini Peanut Butter

Comfort food at its finest. Slather the rich, tangy tahini butter onto these mouthwatering roasted sweet potatoes and you have a perfect pairing. This recipe is easy to make, utterly delicious, and always a hit. Serve as a side dish or with a big salad.

3 large sweet potatoes (any color), halved lengthwise
1 Tbsp olive oil
1 Tbsp toasted white or black sesame seeds or a mix
flaky sea salt and black pepper
lime wedges, to serve

Creamy and zesty tahini peanut butter
2 Tbsp tahini
1 Tbsp peanut butter, smooth or crunchy
5 Tbsp unsalted butter, at room temperature
zest and juice of 1 lime
1 Tbsp soy sauce or tamari
2 tsp toasted sesame oil

1 Preheat the oven to 400°F. Line a baking sheet with parchment paper.

2 Place the halved sweet potatoes on the baking sheet and drizzle with the olive oil. Roast for 15–20 minutes, until lightly charred around the edges and soft in the middle.

3 Meanwhile, make the creamy and zesty tahini peanut butter: in a bowl, combine the tahini, peanut butter, butter, lime juice and zest, soy sauce, and sesame oil, and mix well.

4 Transfer the cooked sweet potatoes to a serving plate and spread the tahini peanut butter over the top of each potato half. Season with sea salt and black pepper, scatter with toasted sesame seeds, and serve with lime wedges.

Tips If gluten is an issue for you, ensure you use tamari, a version of soy sauce made without wheat.

For more crunch, dice the sweet potatoes before roasting.

For an elevated sauce, stir a tablespoon of miso into the tahini peanut butter.

Make extra tahini butter and add it to your favorite roasted veg or rice bowls.

 8   5 mins   15–20 mins   Up to 3 days   Up to 1 month   **GF**

Carrot Pecan Cake and Orange Drizzle

I'm often asked to share carrot recipes, especially carrot cake recipes. I guess people like carrot cake. I aim to please, so here's a super-moist cake with a sweet, citrusy drizzle, making this my best carrot cake yet.

butter, for greasing (see note
  on page 16)
2½ cups all-purpose flour
2 tsp baking powder
1 tsp baking soda
1 tsp salt
1 tsp ground cinnamon
1 tsp ground ginger
1 tsp ground cardamom
¼ tsp ground nutmeg
½ cup pecans, crushed

Wet ingredients
1 cup soy milk
½ cup applesauce
⅓ cup light brown sugar
zest of 1 orange, reserving the juice for
  the drizzle
4½ Tbsp maple syrup
4 Tbsp vegetable oil
2 medium carrots, finely grated

Orange drizzle
1 cup confectioners' sugar
2 Tbsp orange juice

1 Preheat the oven to 350°F. Butter a 10-inch Bundt or other pan.

2 Sift all the dry ingredients, apart from the pecans, into a large mixing bowl.

3 In another bowl, whisk together the soy milk, applesauce, light brown sugar, orange zest, maple syrup, and oil.

4 Make a well in the middle of the flour mixture and pour in the milk mixture. Using a rubber spatula or wooden spoon, gently fold together until no streaks of flour remain. Add the grated carrot and pecans to the bowl and gently fold in.

5 Carefully pour the batter into the prepared pan. Smooth the top, using the back of a spoon. Bake the cake for 30–32 minutes, or until it is cooked all the way through: a skewer inserted into the cake should come out clean.

6 Place the cake—still in its pan—on a wire rack and leave to cool for 10 minutes. Place a cutting board on the exposed side of the cake and carefully and confidently flip it over, then gently remove the pan. Place the cake back on the wire rack to cool completely.

7 For the orange drizzle, mix the confectioners' sugar and half the orange juice in a bowl, adding more orange juice to get your preferred consistency. Drizzle the orange glaze over the cake.

Tip Store in an airtight container at room temperature for up to 3 days, or (without the drizzle) in the fridge for up to 7 days.

 8 20 mins 30 mins 7 days Up to 1 month

2- Grains

Rice
Mixed Grains
Pasta
Bread

Roasted Fennel and Quinoa Salad with Apple and Tahini

My niece is a little over two years old and she loves talking with me about all things food and cooking! I made this fennel and quinoa salad for her christening, and it was a major hit! It's a great recipe to make ahead to take on picnics or pack into a lunch box for work. To add more bulk, add some baked tofu or crispy chickpeas.

½ cup quinoa, soaked for 10–15 minutes, then rinsed
1 cup water
1 small fennel, thinly sliced, reserving fronds to garnish
2 Tbsp olive oil
1 Tbsp tahini
zest and juice of ½ lemon
2 tsp Dijon mustard
1 apple, cored and cut into half-moon slices
½ cucumber, diced
2 Tbsp chopped fresh dill
2 Tbsp chopped fresh mint
¼ cup toasted chopped nuts or seeds
salt and black pepper

1 Put the quinoa, water, and a pinch of salt in a pan over medium heat. Bring to a boil and simmer, uncovered, until all of the liquid has been absorbed, 10–15 minutes. Set aside to cool.

2 Meanwhile, preheat the oven to 400°F. Line a baking sheet with parchment paper.

3 Toss the fennel with 1 tablespoon of the olive oil and season with salt and pepper. Spread out on the baking sheet and roast for 12–14 minutes, tossing halfway through, until the fennel is lightly charred and the edges are golden. Set aside to cool.

4 Meanwhile, in a small jar or bowl, add the remaining olive oil, the tahini, lemon juice, lemon zest, and mustard; close the lid and shake vigorously, or whisk until smooth.

5 Fluff the cooled quinoa with a fork into a large bowl. Add the roasted fennel, the apple and cucumber, the herbs, and some of the toasted nuts or seeds. Drizzle the tahini sauce over and toss until combined. Garnish with the remaining nuts or seeds and the reserved fennel fronds.

Tips Don't add the dressing until you're ready to serve.

If the roasted fennel is wet, pat dry with a paper towel to remove excess water.

 4–8   15 mins   15 mins   Up to 3 days   Up to 1 month   **GF**

Zesty and Herby Summer Orzo Salad

Fast and friendly, this vibrant pasta salad is super-easy to make, and it's great for using up leftover fresh herbs and feta. Perfect for cooling you down on hot summer days, as a speedy midweek meal or a summer side dish for picnics.

⅓ cups orzo or any short pasta or grain
1 cup frozen peas
1 Tbsp extra-virgin olive oil
zest and juice of 1 lemon
3 baby cucumbers, diced
2 Tbsp chopped fresh mint
2 Tbsp chopped fresh dill
2 Tbsp chopped fresh parsley
¼ cup crumbled feta (see note
   on page 16)
generous pinch of salt
¼ tsp black pepper
lemon wedges, to serve

1 Bring a large pan of salted water to a boil, add the orzo, and cook for 8–10 minutes, or until al dente. Drain, run under cold water and drain well, then transfer to a large serving bowl.

2 Meanwhile, put the frozen peas in a bowl and cover with freshly boiled water; leave for 1–2 minutes until bright green. Drain and run the peas under cold water for 30–45 seconds. Drain again and set aside.

3 Drizzle the olive oil, lemon juice, and lemon zest over the cooked orzo. Add all the remaining ingredients and toss until well combined. Chill until ready to serve. Serve on a large plate, with lemon wedges.

Tip Use gluten-free pasta if you prefer.

 4–8   5 mins   15 mins   Up to 5 days

Crunchy Butter Rice, Cherries, and Toasted Hazelnuts

This is my take on a tahdig—an incredible Persian crispy rice dish. Jeweled with tart dried cherries, hazelnuts, onion, red pepper, and fresh thyme, it's a real showstopper of a meal. Flip it over in front of your guests to reveal the delicious crunchy rice on top. You are going to have to fight the urge to stir the rice when it's cooking—trust the process!

1½ cups basmati rice
6 Tbsp butter (see note on page 16)
1 Tbsp olive oil
1 onion, finely chopped
1 red pepper, seeded, thinly sliced
½ cup dried tart cherries, raisins, or golden raisins
1 Tbsp ground coriander
salt

To garnish
⅓ cup toasted hazelnuts, chopped
fresh thyme sprigs

1   Rinse and wash the rice in a large bowl of cold water. Change the water frequently until clear. Bring a large pan of salted water to a boil, add the rice, and boil for 3–4 minutes, until al dente. Drain the rice in a sieve, transfer to a bowl, and set aside.

2   In a non-stick frying pan, melt 2 tablespoons of the butter with the olive oil over medium heat. Add the onion and a generous pinch of salt, and cook, stirring often, for 6–8 minutes, until soft and golden. Add the red pepper and cook, stirring occasionally, for 5–7 minutes, until soft and lightly charred around the edges. Transfer the onion and red pepper to the bowl of rice, add the dried cherries and coriander, and toss to combine.

3   Melt 3 tablespoons of the butter in a heavy-bottomed pan or Dutch oven over medium heat. Spread the rice mixture in the pan in an even layer and pat down lightly. Using the handle of a wooden spoon, make four or five holes in the rice and add the remaining butter, cut into small pieces, to the holes. Cook the rice, uncovered and without stirring, for 4–5 minutes.

Continued   →

 4–8   15 mins   45 mins–1 hour   1 day   Up to 1 month   **GF**

Continued $\longrightarrow$

4 Reduce the heat and cover the pan with a clean cloth and a lid; carefully fold the cloth corners up and over the lid. Cook the rice over low heat for 30–35 minutes. Check after 20–25 minutes to see if the rice smells toasty, but not burnt. Do not be tempted to stir. Remove from the heat and let it stand for 10 minutes.

5 Fluff the rice using a fork and transfer it to a serving bowl. Using a spatula, gently remove the crusty bottom and add it to the rice. Or if you feel inclined, place the top of a large plate over the pan, grab the handles of the pan while holding the plate in place, and in one confident motion flip it over so that the pan is on top. Remove the pan slowly for dramatic effect. Garnish with toasted hazelnuts and small sprigs of fresh thyme.

"What's in the Fridge?" Fried Rice

A surprising ingredient people often ask me about is fresh corn on the cob! This summery fried rice, coated in a peanut-sesame-lime sauce, is the perfect way to celebrate it—and fried rice is also the best vehicle for using up whatever you have lurking in the bottom of your fridge. Any veg will work here, and you can use canned corn if you don't have fresh.

2 large ears of corn, husked
1 Tbsp vegetable oil
4 spring onions, thinly sliced on the diagonal
1 Tbsp butter (see note on page 16)
1 large carrot, not peeled, grated
1 cup leftover cooked rice
3 Tbsp soy sauce or tamari
2 Tbsp peanut butter, or any seed or nut butter
1 tsp toasted sesame oil
1 tsp maple syrup
zest and juice of ½ lime

To serve
1 Tbsp finely snipped fresh chives
1–2 tsp toasted sesame seeds
¼ cup toasted peanuts, crushed

1   Bring a pan of water to a boil, add the corn, and cook until tender, about 5 minutes. Drain and leave to cool. Cut the corn kornels off the cobs and set them aside in a bowl.

2   Heat the oil in a large non-stick frying pan over medium heat. Set aside some spring onion to garnish and add the remaining spring onions to the frying pan; cook for about 2 minutes, stirring occasionally, until soft and lightly browned. Add the corn kernels and butter, stir, and cook for 2–3 minutes.

3   Add the carrot and rice to the pan, stir so that the rice covers the bottom of the pan, then cook undisturbed for 4–5 minutes until the rice begins to crisp.

4   Meanwhile, in a small jar or bowl, add the soy sauce, peanut butter, sesame oil, maple syrup, and lime juice; close the lid and shake vigorously, or whisk until smooth.

5   Pour the sauce over the rice mixture. Stir well to coat, and cook for about 1 minute until the rice is glossy.

6   Serve hot, topped with the lime zest, reserved spring onion, chives, sesame seeds, and crushed peanuts.

Tips Tamari is a gluten-free version of soy sauce.

Save the cobs to add to a veg stock (page 260).

If you like things spicy, add chili sauce.

Double or triple all the ingredients to serve more people.

 2   10 mins   20 mins   1 day   Up to 1 month

Baked Sun-Dried Tomato Rice with a Golden Pastry Lid

Inspired by incredible Indian feasts, this showstopper of a dish is perfect for sharing with friends and family at your next celebration. Breaking through the golden, crispy pastry reveals what's been cooking underneath, and tomatoes are the hero of this biryani-style pie! I've used two types of tomatoes: fresh for texture and sweetness, and sun-dried for a luxurious, umami intensity. It's all cooled down by a creamy raita and crunchy cucumber salad.

1½ cups basmati rice
4½ Tbsp butter, plus more for greasing (see note on page 16)
3 onions, thinly sliced
1 Tbsp garam masala
3 Tbsp vegetable oil or ghee
3 garlic cloves, sliced thinly
1 Tbsp grated fresh ginger
1 Tbsp ground coriander
1 tsp ground turmeric
1 tsp ground cumin
6 plum tomatoes, roughly chopped
4 oz sun-dried tomatoes, sliced in half
½ small head of cauliflower, roughly chopped (save the leaves to use them in my Cauliflower Ragù on page 146)
½ cup yogurt (I use coconut)
1 sheet puff pastry
2 tsp milk, for brushing (I use oat milk)
1 Tbsp olive oil, for brushing
1 tsp nigella seeds
1 tsp cumin seeds
½ tsp brown mustard seeds
salt and black pepper

To serve
small bunch of mint, roughly chopped
raita

Tip Great for big gatherings, try serving this with my Loaded Nachos (page 19) or for a more relaxed evening, with Roasted Fennel and Quinoa Salad (page 50).

1 Rinse the rice under cold running water until the water runs clear. Tip into a saucepan, cover with 2½ cups cold water, bring to a boil, then reduce to a simmer. Cover and cook for 10 minutes, then remove from the heat and leave with the lid on to steam for 10 minutes.

2 Meanwhile, melt the butter in a large saucepan over medium heat. Add the onions and a generous pinch of salt. Cook for 8–10 minutes, stirring often, until soft and translucent. Stir in the garam masala and cook for 1 minute, then set aside.

3 In a large saucepan over medium heat, warm the oil and fry the garlic and ginger for 1–2 minutes, until fragrant. Stir in the spices and cook for 1 minute. Add the plum tomatoes and sun-dried tomatoes, stir until well combined, and cook for 1 minute. Stir in the cauliflower and cook for 8–10 minutes, until the cauliflower is slightly soft. Stir in the yogurt until incorporated, season with salt and black pepper, then remove from the heat.

4 Grease a 9-inch deep-dish pie plate or baking dish with a little butter. Spoon in half of the tomato mixture, then half the rice, then repeat, using up the rest of the tomatoes and rice, so you finish with a layer of rice. Top with the jammy onions.

Continued →

6 | 25 mins | 45–50 mins | Up to 5 days | Up to 1 month

Continued $\longrightarrow$

5 Unroll the pastry sheet and cut to the size of the dish with a slight overhang. Place the pastry sheet over the top of the dish, crimp the edges, and cut 3 or 4 small holes into the surface with a knife to release the steam as it cooks. In a small bowl, mix the oat milk and olive oil, and brush over the pastry. Scatter with the nigella, cumin, and brown mustard seeds.

6 Bake for 25 minutes, until the pastry is golden brown and crispy. Remove from oven and allow to cool for 5 minutes before cracking open the lid at the table. Garnish with the mint and serve with raita.

Golden Split Peas with Herby Rice

A super-easy and satisfying recipe that you can dress up with amazing toppings like toasted coconut flakes, punchy Pickled Red Onion, cool yogurt, and a pop of fresh herbs. If you have the patience or self-control, leave the split peas to sit for 12 hours or overnight to let the spices work their magic, and then reheat to serve. If (like me) you don't have self-control or are too hungry, aim to let them sit for 5–10 minutes before serving.

2 Tbsp vegetable oil
1 onion, finely chopped
1-inch piece fresh ginger, not peeled, finely grated
3 garlic cloves, finely grated
1 cup red or yellow split peas, rinsed well and drained
2 tsp ground coriander
1 tsp cumin seeds, toasted
1 tsp ground turmeric
¼ tsp ground cinnamon
4 cups water or veg stock
salt and black pepper

Herby rice
2 Tbsp butter (see note on page 16)
2 Tbsp chopped fresh cilantro stems
2 Tbsp chopped fresh mint stems
1 cup long-grain rice (white or brown)

To serve
4 Tbsp coconut flakes
zest of 1 lime
yogurt (I use coconut)
Pickled Red Onion (page 267)
chopped fresh cilantro and mint

1 Heat the oil in a large saucepan over medium heat. Cook the onion for 5–8 minutes, until soft, stirring frequently. Add the ginger and garlic, season with salt and pepper, and cook, still stirring, for 30 seconds. Stir in the split peas, ground coriander, cumin seeds, turmeric, and cinnamon for 30–45 seconds, until you can smell all those delicious aromatics. Pour in half the water and bring to a boil. Reduce the heat to medium-low and simmer for 10–15 minutes, until the split peas are tender. Cover and keep warm over low heat.

2 To make the herby rice, melt the butter in a medium saucepan over medium heat. Add the herb stems and cook, stirring frequently, for 2–3 minutes, until lightly brown and fragrant. Add the rice and cook, stirring occasionally, for about 2 minutes, until the rice is lightly toasted. Pour in the remaining water, bring to a boil, then reduce the heat and simmer for 10–15 minutes, until the liquid has been absorbed. Remove from the heat and cover with a lid.

3 Meanwhile, in a small frying pan over medium heat, toast the coconut flakes for 2–3 minutes, stirring often, until lightly browned. Set aside.

4 Serve the herby rice topped with lime zest and the toasted coconut flakes. Spoon the golden split peas alongside, and top with yogurt, the pickled red onion, and lots of chopped herbs.

Tips Cook the split peas and serve the next day—or enjoy amazing leftovers!

Serve with my Fragrant Flatbreads (page 206).

 4   10 mins   30–45 mins   1–3 days   Up to 1 month

One-Pot Pantry Pasta

One of my most popular dishes and for good reason—it's a one-pot pasta dish, and you don't even need a colander to strain the pasta! It's delicious, satisfying, takes only 20 minutes, and is made with ingredients you probably already have at home. Great for lunch, weeknight meals with the family, or whenever you're feeling lazy. You will be making this time and time again.

1 Tbsp olive oil
2 garlic cloves, finely chopped
½ cup cooked lentils (canned are fine)
¼ cup pitted green olives, sliced
1 Tbsp tomato purée
pinch of red pepper flakes
1 (14-oz) can chopped tomatoes
large handful of baby spinach
6½ oz spaghetti, linguine, bucatini, or
    any long pasta
2½ cups water or veg stock
large handful of fresh basil and parsley,
    torn or roughly chopped
flaky sea salt and black pepper
extra-virgin olive oil, to serve

1   Heat the oil in a large non-stick pot over medium-low heat and fry the garlic for 1–2 minutes until fragrant and lightly brown, stirring occasionally.

2   Add the lentils, olives, and tomato purée, season with salt, black pepper, and red pepper flakes, and cook, stirring, for another 2–3 minutes. Add the tomatoes and spinach and cook for 3–4 minutes, stirring until the spinach is soft and the sauce begins to bubble slightly.

3   Add the pasta and carefully pour in the water, stir, then increase the heat to medium-high and simmer for 8–10 minutes, stirring occasionally, until the pasta is al dente. If you prefer a thicker sauce, let it sit for 5 minutes before serving.

4   Serve in bowls, garnished with the torn or roughly chopped herbs, a drizzle of extra-virgin olive oil, and a pinch of flaky sea salt.

Tips Use gluten-free pasta if you prefer.

Double or triple all the ingredients to serve more people.

 2   5 mins   15–20 mins   Up to 3 days   Up to 1 month

Grains

Curried Couscous with Sticky Butternut and Cilantro Chutney

Wonderfully spiced chickpeas and sweet and sticky roasted butternut squash are topped with a punchy herby-lime-ginger-chile chutney. This Israeli couscous platter has intense flavors and textures coming at you from every direction!

1 butternut squash
2 Tbsp maple syrup
3 Tbsp olive oil
1 Tbsp cumin seeds
10 oz Israeli couscous
1 large onion, finely diced
2 tsp grated fresh ginger
2 garlic cloves, thinly sliced
2 Tbsp curry powder
1 Tbsp ground coriander
zest and juice of 1 lime
1 (14-oz) can chickpeas, drained (save the liquid for meringues, see page 228)
salt and black pepper

To serve
4 Tbsp yogurt (see note on page 16)
6 Tbsp roughly chopped toasted cashews

The chutney
large handful of fresh cilantro
large handful of fresh mint
zest and juice of 2 limes
1 tsp grated fresh ginger
6–8 curry leaves (optional)
3 spring onions, roughly chopped
1–2 green chiles, depending on how much heat you like (remove the seeds if you like it less hot)

Tips Israeli couscous has an amazing texture but go ahead and swap it out for any grain you need to use up.

Pumpkin and celeriac will work well instead of the butternut.

1 Preheat the oven to 400°F.

2 Cut the squash in half lengthwise. Remove the seeds and set aside (you can rinse them and then toast them as a snack). Slice the squash halves into half-moons. Place the squash on a baking sheet. In a small bowl, mix the maple syrup and 1 tablespoon of the oil. Drizzle over the squash and scatter with the cumin seeds. Season with salt and roast for 20 minutes, until soft and sticky. Turn on the broiler and cook for 5–10 minutes further, until the squash is a little charred.

3 Bring a saucepan of salted water to a boil, and cook the couscous according to package instructions. Drain well and set aside.

4 Meanwhile, heat the remaining oil in a large frying pan over a medium heat. Fry the onion and ginger with a generous pinch of salt and cook for about 5 minutes, until softened. Add the garlic, curry powder, and coriander, and cook for 1 minute further, stirring often. Remove from the heat, add the zest and juice of the lime, then tip in the chickpeas and couscous and toss well. Season to taste with salt and black pepper.

5 To make the chutney, purée all the ingredients in a food processor until smooth.

6 To serve, pile the curried couscous onto a platter or into bowls and top with the sticky roasted squash. Drizzle with a little yogurt, then a little of the chutney. Scatter with toasted cashews and serve.

 4–6
 20 mins
 25–30 mins
 Up to 5 days
 Up to 1 month

Roasted Root Veg Sub Sandwiches

I come from Connecticut, a state that is known for its BIG sandwiches. My dad also owned a series of sandwich shops, so I grew up surrounded by sandwiches! In this packed-out sub–which has become my ultimate go-to sandwich–mixed root veg and cream cheese are drizzled with an intensely herby, tangy sauce. There's no pausing when you eat this sandwich; you'll just keep going in for more.

2 lb mixed root veggies (I used carrots, parsnips, beets, and celeriac)
2 Tbsp olive oil
1 Tbsp cumin seeds
4–6 sub rolls
4 Tbsp cream cheese or crème fraîche (see note on page 16)
2 Tbsp mayonnaise
1 tsp mustard

The green sauce
3½ oz leafy fresh green herbs (I used a mix of parsley, cilantro, dill, and chives)
zest and juice of 1–2 lemons
2 Tbsp drained capers, roughly chopped
3 Tbsp olive oil, plus more if needed
salt and black pepper

1   Preheat the oven to 400°F.

2   Cut your carrots and parsnips into batons; slice the beets into ⅜-inch pieces, and the celeriac into ⅜-inch half-moons and then into quarters. Add the carrots, parsnips, and celeriac to a roasting pan and toss with 1 tablespoon of the olive oil and half the cumin seeds. Add the beets to another roasting pan and toss with the remaining olive oil and cumin. Roast the veg for about 45 minutes, until very soft on the inside and crispy on the outside; you should be able to poke a fork easily into the veg.

3   Meanwhile, in a food processor or blender, process the herbs, lemon zest and juice, and the capers to make a thick paste. Stir in the olive oil. Season with salt and black pepper, adding more lemon juice and/or olive oil if required.

4   Slice your sub rolls in half horizontally. In a small bowl, mix the cream cheese with the mayonnaise and mustard. Spread the rolls with the creamy mixture, pile the vegetables on top, then drizzle with the green sauce. Top with the other half of the sub rolls, pressing them down, then cut into quarters. Eat immediately or wrap up and take on a picnic!

Tip You can keep the roasted veg, stored separately, in the fridge for the next day.

 4–6   10 mins   45 mins   Up to 1 day

Super "Meatball" Sliders

Burgers are one of the dishes people often say they miss the most when they switch to a plant-based diet, but these tasty sliders prove you can still enjoy all those delicious flavors! Perfect for parties, get-togethers, and big events with friends and family. Liquid smoke adds a char-grilled taste but it's not essential to the recipe–or you can cook them on the grill instead. These are great packed into the Potato Rolls on page 38.

8 oz chestnut mushrooms, finely chopped (or use cremini mushrooms)
1 (14-oz) can cannellini beans, drained and rinsed
1 small onion, finely chopped
4 garlic cloves, finely grated
1¼–1½ cups breadcrumbs (homemade from a stale loaf)
1 cup fresh parsley, finely chopped
½ tsp dried rosemary
¼ tsp fennel seeds
1 tsp Worcestershire sauce
1 Tbsp soy sauce or tamari
½ tsp liquid smoke
3 Tbsp vegetable oil
1¼ cups prepared tomato sauce or passata (or my Simplest Tomato Sauce, page 87)
12 bread rolls
4 oz mozzarella, shredded (see note on page 16)
2 Tbsp butter, melted
1 Tbsp grated parmesan
½ tsp sugar
salt and black pepper

Tips If you need gluten-free sliders, ensure you use gluten-free bread and breadcrumbs, and tamari rather than soy sauce.

Look for vegan Worcestershire sauce if you prefer.

1 In a food processor, pulse the mushrooms, beans, onion, 3 garlic cloves, 1¼ cups of the breadcrumbs, the parsley (reserving 1 tablespoon for the topping), rosemary, fennel seeds, Worcestershire sauce, soy sauce, liquid smoke, and ½ teaspoon each of salt and black pepper until combined, but go slowly so that the mixture doesn't turn mushy. If it seems a little mushy, add some more breadcrumbs.

2 Line a baking sheet or large plate with parchment paper. Roll the mushroom mixture into 12 golf-ball–sized pieces, place them on the lined baking sheet or plate, then chill in the fridge to firm up for 30–45 minutes.

3 Preheat the oven to 350°F. Line a 9 x 12-inch roasting pan with parchment paper.

4 Heat the vegetable oil in a large frying pan over medium-high heat until shimmering. Carefully place the balls in the pan and cook for about 10 minutes, until browned all over. Pour in the tomato sauce and cook for a further 2 minutes, gently stirring to coat the balls.

5 Slice the bread rolls in half and place the bottom halves in the lined roasting pan. Place one meatball on each half with 2–3 tablespoons of the sauce, then add the mozzarella (about 1 tablespoon on each roll). Cover with the tops of the rolls.

6 In a small bowl, combine the melted butter, parmesan, sugar, and the remaining garlic and parsley. Season with salt and black pepper. Brush the tops of the rolls with the sweet and salty butter mixture.

7 Bake in the oven for 15 minutes, or until the bread is golden brown. Remove from the oven and leave to cool slightly before serving.

 12 sliders

 20 mins, plus 30+ mins chilling

 30 mins

 1–2 days

 Up to 1 month

Grains

Nut Roast Cake with All the Trimmings

I first made this nut roast when we were visiting family at Christmas. My wife and I were the only vegans in the house, but there wasn't enough for us to have seconds as the plate was wiped clean! Now I always make three so we can finally enjoy leftovers on Boxing Day. It's definitely a crowd-pleaser for vegans and non-vegans alike.

1¼ lb carrots, preferably heirloom, halved lengthwise and cut into 2–3 inch batons
2 sweet potatoes
3 Tbsp olive oil
2 Tbsp butter (see note on page 16)
7 oz fresh mushrooms, sliced
2 garlic cloves, finely chopped
1 Tbsp ground coriander
1 tsp ground cinnamon
1 tsp grated nutmeg
1 tsp ground cumin
a few sprigs of fresh thyme
2 Tbsp flaxseed or chia seeds
3 Tbsp water
3½ oz mixed nuts, toasted
1 (8-oz) package quick-cook mixed grains (such as TruRoots)
1 (14-oz) can lentils, drained and rinsed
1 Tbsp Marmite yeast extract (or sub in soy sauce)
3 Tbsp roughly chopped fresh parsley
3 Tbsp roughly chopped fresh sage
2 Tbsp nutritional yeast
1 cup breadcrumbs
salt and black pepper

To serve
Best Roasted Potatoes (page 33) (I'd probably make double the quantity!)
roasted Brussels sprouts
gravy
cranberry sauce

1   Preheat the oven to 425°F.

2   Place the carrots and sweet potatoes on a baking sheet and rub with a little of the olive oil and some salt. Cook in the oven for 35–40 minutes, or until very soft.

3   Meanwhile, heat the remaining olive oil and the butter in a large frying pan over high heat. Once hot, add the sliced mushrooms and a big pinch of salt and black pepper. Fry for 5–7 minutes until all the liquid has been released from the mushrooms and they're soft and golden. Add the garlic and spices, cook for 1 minute, stir in the thyme, then tip into a large bowl.

4   In a small bowl, mix the flaxseed with the water and set aside until it turns into a jelly-like consistency.

5   Put half the toasted nuts in a food processor or blender along with half the mixed grains, half the lentils, a splash of water, and the Marmite, and blend into a paste. Roughly chop the remaining nuts and add them to the mushrooms, along with the remaining grains and lentils.

6   When the sweet potato is cooked, add 1½ potatoes to the blender and blend again. Roughly chop the remaining half a potato, and add to the mushrooms. Preheat the oven to 350°F.

Continued ⟶

 8
 20 min
1 hour 55 mins –2 hours 5 min
 Up to 1 week
 Up to 1 month

Continued $\longrightarrow$

7 Line the base of a 9-inch springform pan with a circle of parchment paper. Lay the carrots, cut side down, in the pan (I like to lay them in alternating directions to ensure as few gaps as possible).

8 Combine the flaxseed mixture and the chopped herbs with the mushrooms, then add the blender mixture, along with the nutritional yeast and breadcrumbs. Stir everything together; the mixture should be thick. Tip into the pan, being careful not to move the carrots too much. Tap the base of the pan on a flat surface to make sure everything is settled in the pan.

9 Cover with foil and bake for 1 hour. Remove the foil and cook for a further 20–25 minutes, until evenly golden. Remove from the oven and allow to cool a little, then turn out onto a plate. Peel back the parchment paper to reveal the amazing carrot surface. Slice and serve with all the roast dinner trimmings.

Tips You can prep the mixture in advance and pull everything together in the morning.

It's freezer friendly, too: make it up to a month in advance, then bake it in the oven to heat through on the day.

It's best if your carrots aren't too thick for this.

Buttery Herb Stuffing

I've found that stuffing recipes often have loads of complicated steps, so this one cuts out all the fuss—and uses up leftover bread in the process. Easy to pull together and flavored with an abundance of fresh herbs, it takes (some of) the stress out of festive cooking. If you have any leftovers, check out the stuffed mushroom recipe on page 246.

1 lb sourdough (or other) bread, torn into ¾–1-inch pieces
½ cup plus 1 Tbsp butter (see note on page 16)
About 5 stalks celery, finely chopped
1 medium onion, finely chopped
4 garlic cloves, finely chopped
½ cup dry white wine
2 Tbsp chopped fresh rosemary
2 Tbsp chopped fresh thyme
2 Tbsp chopped fresh sage
1 cup veg stock
⅓ cup cold water
2 Tbsp cornstarch
salt and black pepper

1 Preheat the oven to its lowest setting. Place the bread on a baking sheet and bake for 15 minutes, or until the bread is dried out on the surface.

2 Melt the butter in a frying pan over medium heat. Add the celery and onion and cook for about 10 minutes, stirring occasionally, until soft. Stir in the garlic and cook for 1 minute, until fragrant. Add the wine and herbs, increase the heat to bring the wine to a simmer, and cook for 5 minutes, until reduced. Add the stock, bring to a simmer, and cook for 5 minutes.

3 Meanwhile, in a small bowl, stir the water and cornstarch until there are no clumps.

4 Stir the cornstarch mixture into the stock and cook for 1–2 minutes, until the mixture thickens slightly. Remove from the heat.

5 Increase the oven temperature to 350°F.

6 Put the dried bread in a large baking dish and pour over the onion and celery mixture. Stir until the bread is evenly coated and season with salt and black pepper. Cover with foil and bake for 20 minutes. Remove the foil and bake for a further 18–20 minutes, until dried out on top and crispy around the edges.

7 Remove from the oven and leave to cool slightly before serving.

Tips Skip the first step and let the bread dry out 2–3 days in advance.

Use gluten-free bread if you prefer.

 8   15 mins   1 hour 20 mins   Up to 7 days   Up to 3 months

Rich Ribollita

This classic Italian soup is traditionally made from leftovers, which is music to my stomach! A hug in a bowl, every mouthful fills you with warmth, love, and goodness. It's very flexible—any kind of beans will work, add sweet potato or pumpkin or regular potatoes, stir in spinach at the end, swap celery for fennel. . . . Make it your own with whatever you have knocking around. Great as leftovers the next day, too—and, most important, it is freezer friendly.

12 oz sourdough (or other) bread, torn or cut into large chunks
6 Tbsp extra-virgin olive oil, plus more for drizzling
1 onion, chopped
3 carrots, cut into ⅜-inch pieces
2 celery stalks, cut into ⅜-inch pieces
4 garlic cloves, thinly sliced
2 (14-oz) cans chopped tomatoes
1 Tbsp tomato purée
½ tsp red pepper flakes
½ tsp dried thyme
½ tsp dried oregano
2 (14-oz) cans cannellini beans, drained and rinsed
4 cups veg stock
small bunch of kale, leaves stripped from stems and roughly chopped
salt and black pepper
1 cup grated parmesan, to serve (see note on page 16)

1   Preheat the oven to 350°F.

2   Toss the bread with 3 tablespoons of olive oil, then season with salt and pepper. Gently squeeze the bread to allow the oil to work into all the nooks and crannies. Bake for 8–10 minutes, until the bread is crispy and golden brown around the edges.

3   Meanwhile, heat the remaining olive oil in a large ovenproof casserole or saucepan over medium heat. Add the onion, carrots, celery, and garlic and cook, stirring occasionally, for 8–10 minutes, until all the vegetables are soft. Season with salt.

4   Add the tomatoes, tomato purée, and red pepper flakes and cook, stirring often, for 8–10 minutes, until slightly thickened. Add the dried thyme and oregano, cannellini beans, and stock, bring to a simmer, and cook for 5–7 minutes, stirring occasionally. Stir in the kale and cook for about 5 minutes, until the kale is very soft and wilted.

5   Add 1–2 large handfuls of the crunchy bread, stir, then season to taste with salt and pepper. Ladle into bowls, topped with more of the crunchy bread, a drizzle of olive oil, and some grated parmesan.

Tips This can be made in an Instant Pot, slow cooker, or on the stovetop.

*To make in advance—or to store leftovers—don't add the crunchy bread until ready to eat.

Use gluten-free bread if you prefer.

Use the kale stems for Fridge Greens Fusilli (page 160) or Stems and Herbs Pesto (page 156).

 4   15 mins   30 mins   1–2 days*   Up to 1 month

Brown Butter and Crispy Sage Mac and Peas

This is an adult version of everyone's childhood favorite—mac and cheese! The puffed cereal and breadcrumbs give it an incredible texture on top. Perfect as a midweek dinner or serve as a side dish.

1¼ cups bread cubes (any type, preferably slightly stale)
4½ Tbsp butter (see note on page 16)
½ cup all-purpose flour
3 cups milk (I use oat)
1 lb macaroni or pasta shells
1 cup shredded cheddar cheese
⅔ cup frozen peas
1 generous cup puffed rice cereal, crushed
3 Tbsp chopped fresh parsley
3 Tbsp olive oil
salt and black pepper

Brown butter–sage sauce
4½ Tbsp butter
3 Tbsp roughly chopped fresh sage

Tips It's best to use bread that is not baked fresh that day.

Keep the crusts on the bread to waste less.

Breadcrumbs can be made in advance and kept in the freezer.

1   Preheat the oven to 300°F.

2   Pulse the bread in a food processor for a few seconds to a crumb texture. Spread the crumbs on a baking sheet in a single layer and bake for 8–10 minutes, until lightly toasted and dry. Remove from the oven and set aside.

3   Meanwhile, melt the butter in a large saucepan over medium heat. Add the flour, whisking continuously, and cook for 1 minute. Whisk in the milk and bring to a boil, then reduce the heat and simmer for 8–10 minutes, stirring often, to a silky, glossy sauce. Season, then remove from the heat.

4   Meanwhile, bring a large pan of water to a boil and cook the macaroni for 4 minutes. Drain well.

5   Increase the oven temperature to 400°F.

6   Toss the macaroni and three-quarters of the cheddar into a shallow baking dish. Pour over the sauce (do not stir) and cover with foil. Bake for about 15 minutes, until the macaroni is slightly tender.

7   Meanwhile, make the brown butter. Heat the butter in a frying pan over medium heat. Add the sage and cook for 3–5 minutes, stirring occasionally, until the butter turns brown and has a nutty aroma. Remove from the heat.

8   Place the frozen peas in a colander and run under hot water for 30 seconds, then drain and set aside until dry. Toss the peas in the sage butter and set aside.

9   In a bowl, toss the breadcrumbs and crushed cereal with the parsley and olive oil.

10 Remove the foil. Sprinkle over the remaining cheddar, pour over the brown butter and peas, and scatter on the breadcrumbs. Bake, uncovered, for 8–10 minutes, until the edges start bubbling and the top is golden. Cool slightly before serving.

 4–8   15 mins   40 mins   Up to 5 days   Up to 3 months

BYOB (Build Your Own Bruschetta)

Easy to make and one of my favorite ways to use up leftover bread and tomatoes, these can be assembled on the spot—and I love getting other people involved in cooking! A little different from a traditional bruschetta, this has white beans for a chunky texture. To lift the sweetness, try a handful of strawberries or raspberries, too.

1 large crusty baguette
4–6 garlic cloves, peeled and left whole
handful of fresh basil and mint, to serve
good olive oil, to drizzle

Balsamic tomatoes
1 small red onion
zest and juice of 1 lemon
2 Tbsp thick balsamic vinegar
1 cup sun-dried tomatoes
1⅓ cups cherry tomatoes
2 medium heirloom tomatoes
1 (14-oz) can white beans, rinsed and drained
salt and black pepper

1 Make the balsamic tomatoes. Finely chop the red onion and add to a bowl with the lemon zest and juice, the balsamic vinegar, and a big pinch of salt.

2 Roughly chop the sun-dried tomatoes and add to the mixture. Halve the cherry tomatoes and roughly chop the heirloom tomatoes and add both to the bowl. Add the white beans and season with salt and black pepper. Set the tomato mixture in the middle of the table, ready for people to start assembling their bruschetta.

3 Heat the broiler to high. Slice the baguette on an angle and cook the slices for 2–3 minutes on each side, until golden brown. Arrange on a plate and put on the table.

4 Now for the fun part: let everyone use the peeled garlic to rub on their bread, before piling high with the tomato mixture and scattering with fresh herbs. Finally, pass around a nice bottle of olive oil so people can drizzle it all over their bruschetta.

Tip Substitute gluten-free bread for the baguette, if you desire.

 4–6   10 mins   5 mins   Up to 3 days

Sourdough French Toast with Glazed Peaches

When I eat a peach, I always feel as though time seems to slow down. You can't rush eating peaches–they're too juicy and delicious! Grilled with maple syrup, they create a beautiful sticky glaze to serve on top of cinnamon French toast. Change the fruits with the seasons so you can enjoy this all year round–try it with bananas or stewed berries and apples.

2 Tbsp all-purpose flour
1 Tbsp flaxseed meal
1 tsp ground cinnamon
¼ tsp grated nutmeg
1 tsp vanilla extract
1 Tbsp sugar
1 cup oat milk
3 peaches, pits removed, flesh cut into wedges
2–3 Tbsp maple syrup
4 Tbsp butter (see note on page 16)
4 slices of sourdough bread

To serve
1–2 Tbsp yogurt per serving (I use coconut)
½ tsp confectioners' sugar per serving
¼ tsp ground cinnamon per serving

1   In a large bowl, whisk the flour, flaxseed, cinnamon, nutmeg, vanilla extract, and sugar until combined. Slowly pour in the milk, still whisking, to make a very thin batter with no streaks of flour. Set aside.

2   Heat a griddle pan or large frying pan over a high heat. Line the pan with a piece of parchment paper and add the peach wedges. Cook for 6–8 mins, turning halfway, until softened and a little charred. Drizzle the maple syrup over the peaches in the pan, then remove from the heat and transfer to a plate with the paper. (Depending on the size of your pan, you might have to do this in batches.)

3   In a large frying pan, heat 2 tablespoons of the butter over medium-high heat. Dip 2 of the sourdough slices in the batter, really drenching them through, then cook in the butter for 2–3 minutes on each side, until golden and slightly crispy. Repeat with the remaining butter and slices of bread.

4   Top the French toast with the glazed peaches and a dollop of yogurt. Sprinkle with a little confectioners' sugar and cinnamon on each serving.

Tips Experiment with whatever bread you have left over: bagels, croissants, even doughnuts!

Best served hot!

 4   5 mins   10–15 mins   1 week   Up to 1 month

3– Nightshades

Tomato
Eggplant
Pepper

One-Pan Lasagna

If you have Italian heritage, you'll know that breaking pasta is basically blasphemy. But I won't tell if you won't! This one-pan wonder shortcuts your way to a creamy, satisfying beautiful lasagna in less than half the time—plus less washing up, too. Sometimes, life is just too short to layer up lasagna sheets. Keep an eye on the heat and don't have it too high, as it could dry out the pasta before it's cooked through—add a splash or two of water if necessary.

2 Tbsp olive oil
1 onion, finely chopped
2 Tbsp chopped fresh basil, plus stems, chopped separately
2 garlic cloves, finely grated
2⅔ cups cooked black or du Puy lentils (or use canned)
1 cup walnuts, chopped
2 Tbsp tomato purée
1 (14-oz) can chopped tomatoes
½ cup oat milk
½ cup water or veg stock
6 oz dried lasagna sheets
1½ tsp chopped fresh oregano
⅔ cup grated parmesan (see note on page 16)
salt and black pepper
Cheesy Garlic Bread (page 199), to serve

1 Heat the olive oil in a large skillet or heavy-bottomed frying pan over medium heat. Add the onion and basil stems and cook for 5–7 minutes, stirring occasionally, until soft, then season with salt and pepper.

2 Add the garlic, lentils, and walnuts; stir and cook for a further 2 minutes. Add the tomato purée and cook for 1–2 minutes, stirring often, until the mixture thickens and begins to stick to the pan. Stir in the tomatoes, milk, and water.

3 Break the lasagna sheets in half and then in half again. Add the broken lasagna to the sauce, stirring, a little at a time so that they don't cling together. Then reduce the heat and cook, stirring often, for 15–20 minutes or until the pasta is al dente.

4 Divide the lasagna among 4 bowls or plates and sprinkle with fresh basil, oregano, and parmesan. Serve with my cheesy garlic bread.

Tip Use gluten-free pasta if you prefer.

 4   10 mins   25–35 mins   1–2 days   Up to 1 month

Speedy Cherry Tomato Fettuccine

My mom's tomato sauce is incredible, but it's an all-day affair, starting at 7 a.m. on a Saturday and filling the house with slowly roasting onions and garlic until late afternoon. I don't want to be at the stove all day, and so this quick and easy cherry tomato pasta dish with garlic, basil, and red pepper flakes is on the table in under 20 minutes!

1 pint cherry tomatoes
3 Tbsp extra-virgin olive oil
2 garlic cloves, finely grated
4 fresh basil sprigs, tender stems
   chopped and leaves separated
¼ tsp red pepper flakes
1 Tbsp tomato purée
7 oz fettuccine
⅔ cup grated parmesan cheese
   (see note on page 16)
salt and pepper
approx. ⅓ cup Garlic and Lemon
   Pangrattato (page 200), to serve

1   Slice half the cherry tomatoes, leaving the rest of them whole.

2   Warm the olive oil in a large saucepan over medium heat. Once the oil is warm, but not burning, add all the tomatoes and cook for 5–7 minutes, stirring often, until they have lost some of their shape. Add the grated garlic, basil stems, and red pepper flakes. Stir to combine and cook for 1 minute before stirring in the tomato purée. Cook for a further 1 minute, then season with salt and black pepper. Remove from heat.

3   Meanwhile, bring a large saucepan of salted water to a boil. Cook the fettuccine according to the package directions. Drain the pasta, reserving 5 tablespoons of the pasta cooking water.

4   Return the tomatoes to a low heat, add the fettuccine, and stir in 1 tablespoon of the reserved pasta cooking water at a time until the sauce clings to the pasta. Sprinkle in parmesan cheese as you go, tossing in between.

5   Serve the pasta hot, divided into bowls, topped with my garlic and lemon pangrattato and the basil leaves.

Tip Grating in the garlic near the end retains its depth so it doesn't become too sweet.

 2
 5 mins
 12 mins
 Up to 5 days
 Up to 3 months

Simplest Tomato Sauce

This version of homemade sauce takes less than half the time! Grating the tomato first means it's already mostly broken down, so it cooks quickly and results in a much smoother, even sauce. I like to batch-cook this sauce in the summer when tomatoes are in abundance. Last year I turned 45 pounds of tomatoes into sauce and canned it to enjoy in the winter.

2¼ lb large ripe tomatoes
1 Tbsp extra-virgin olive oil
4 garlic cloves, finely grated
1 Tbsp tomato purée
1 bunch of fresh basil, stems chopped
1 Tbsp butter
salt and black pepper

1 First, you're going to grate the tomatoes. Cut a slice off the stem end of each tomato and set the sliced-off bits aside. Pressing the cut side of the tomatoes against the largest holes of a box grater, grate them into a large bowl. Finely chop the sliced-off bits and any pieces of tomato that are too difficult to grate and add them to the bowl.

2 Generously season with salt and black pepper. Gently mix in the olive oil, grated garlic, tomato purée, basil stems, and butter.

3 Into a large saucepan over medium heat, slowly pour the tomato mixture. Cook for 10–12 minutes, stirring often. Remove from the heat and serve immediately, or pour into an airtight container while still warm.

Tips Swap fresh tomatoes for canned tomatoes, skip the grating, and go straight to step 2.

You need only the basil stems for this sauce: use the leaves to garnish when serving with pasta or other dishes.

Make the sauce up to 5 days in advance, or freeze.

 2 lb
 15 mins
 20 mins
 Up to 5 days
 Up to 3 months
GF

One-Tray Baked Gnocchi

Sometimes when I post a new recipe on social media, it really seems to resonate with how everyone's feeling—and this dish was one of those! With millions of views on Instagram, I can see why it's so popular. It's basically a deluxe version of a pasta bake—simple cooking and easy to serve up, with all the flavors merging together as the pasta gets slightly crispy. Try it with your favorite ravioli or tortellini, too.

14 oz frozen gnocchi

3 Tbsp extra-virgin olive oil

1 generous pint cherry tomatoes, chopped

2½ oz mozzarella, shredded (see note on page 16)

3 Tbsp chopped fresh basil leaves, plus stems, chopped separately

4 sausages (e.g., plant-based Italian-style), sliced

4 garlic cloves, finely grated

3 cups leafy greens (e.g., spinach, kale, Swiss chard), roughly chopped

salt and black pepper

1 Preheat the oven to 400°F.

2 Place the gnocchi in a large bowl, cover with boiling water, and leave for 2 minutes. Stir, then drain thoroughly.

3 Add the gnocchi to a large roasting pan, drizzle with the olive oil, then add the tomatoes, mozzarella, basil stems, sausages, garlic, and leafy greens. Toss to combine and season with salt and black pepper.

4 Bake for 20 minutes, until the gnocchi are slightly charred around the edges. Remove from the oven and leave to cool for a few minutes before serving.

5 Serve in bowls, sprinkled with chopped basil.

Tips Swap gnocchi for tortellini or ravioli.

It's also great as leftovers.

 4   10 mins   20 mins   1–3 days   Up to 1 month

Tomato Salad, Tofu Whip, and Garlicky Crumbs

Juicy tomatoes, crunchy garlicky crumbs, and a creamy tofu dressing—I just can't get enough of this in the summer when tomatoes are at their peak. Simple, fresh flavors and subtle heat from the Dijon mustard let the tomatoes shine in all their glory as the stars of the show.

2 lb mixed tomatoes, preferably heirloom
2 slices sourdough bread (stale bread is better)
2 Tbsp olive oil
2 garlic cloves, minced
¼ cup drained capers
zest of 1 lemon
1 Tbsp roughly chopped fresh parsley
salt
1 cup shaved parmesan, to serve (see note on page 16)

Tofu whip
1 (8-oz) block silken tofu
3 Tbsp nutritional yeast
1 Tbsp miso paste
juice of 1 lemon
salt and black pepper

1 Slice the tomatoes and place on a large plate. Season with salt.

2 In a food processor, pulse the bread to form breadcrumbs. Heat a large frying pan over medium heat and dry-fry the breadcrumbs for 2 minutes to remove any moisture. Add the oil and stir to coat the breadcrumbs. Add the garlic and capers, fry for about 2 minutes until golden brown, then transfer to a bowl. Season with salt and stir in the lemon zest and parsley.

3 In a food processor, blend the ingredients for the tofu whip until smooth and slightly thick. Season with salt and black pepper.

4 Spread the whipped tofu on a large platter, arrange the tomatoes on top, and scatter with parmesan shavings and the herby zesty garlicky breadcrumbs.

 4   10 mins   5 mins   Up to 5 days

Salted Tomato Grilled Cheese

This takes grilled cheese sandwiches up a notch. Salting and draining the tomatoes and sliding them into your cooked sandwich just before serving removes some of the moisture and firms up the tomato, meaning you won't end up with a soggy sandwich and a burning-hot tomato slice inside. It also enhances the true sweetness of the tomato.

2 large beefsteak or heirloom tomatoes, thinly sliced
10 oz cheddar cheese, grated (see note on page 16)
2¼ oz pepper jack or other chile-flavored cheese, grated
8 slices sourdough (or other) bread
4 Tbsp butter, softened
4 Tbsp mayo
salt and black pepper

1   Place the tomato slices in a single layer on a wire rack set over a roasting pan. Season with a generous pinch of salt, then leave for 20 minutes to release some of their juices, flipping them over halfway through. Pat the tomato slices dry just before serving.

2   Mix the cheeses to combine evenly.

3   Heat a large frying pan over low heat. Spread 2 slices of bread with butter on one side, then place them butter side down in the frying pan. Spread both slices with mayonnaise, then sprinkle a quarter of the cheeses on top of each slice. Spread a layer of mayonnaise on 2 more slices of bread, then gently press them down on top of the cheese, closing the sandwiches. Cook for about 8 minutes, pressing down with a wide spatula, until the bottom is golden brown. Spread the top of each sandwich with butter, then carefully flip them over and cook until golden brown and crispy.

4   Transfer the sandwiches to plates, then carefully lift up the top slices of bread and insert a few slices of tomato. Press the top slices of bread down lightly again to close the sandwiches and cut them in half.

5   Repeat to make 2 more sandwiches.

Tips How to make the perfect tomato and grilled cheese:

Salt your tomatoes to remove excess liquid; pat them dry and add them just before serving.

Grate the cheeses, for faster and more even melting.

Use gluten-free bread if you prefer.

4   10 mins   30 mins

Quick Gazpacho

Although I'm usually more of a hot-tomato-soup-and-grilled-cheese-sandwich kind of guy, when the sun's out, I always turn to this refreshing chilled gazpacho to cool me down. Nectarine brings out the sweetness of the tomatoes and perfectly balances all the flavors. Go ahead and serve it with the Salted Tomato Grilled Cheese on page 93 for a hot-cold contrast.

1 cucumber
2 large very ripe tomatoes, quartered
1 large red pepper, seeded and
   quartered
1 large ripe nectarine, pit removed,
   halved
1 small shallot, chopped
2 garlic cloves, finely grated
2 Tbsp sherry vinegar
3 Tbsp extra-virgin olive oil, plus more
   for drizzling
salt and black pepper

To serve
⅓ cup cherry tomatoes, thinly sliced
snipped fresh chives

1 Slice 2 inches of the cucumber and set aside for garnish. Roughly chop the remaining cucumber and place in a large bowl with the quartered tomatoes, red pepper, nectarine, shallot, garlic, vinegar, and 1 teaspoon of salt. Gently toss together, then chill in the fridge for at least 30 minutes and up to 4 hours for the flavors to blend.

2 Carefully add the contents of the bowl, including all the juices, to a high-speed blender. Add the olive oil and blend on medium-high speed until smooth. Strain through a wide-mesh sieve into a large bowl or container, then chill for at least 30 minutes, or until ready to serve.

3 Serve the gazpacho topped with sliced cherry tomatoes, the reserved cucumber slices, chives, and a drizzle of olive oil. Season with salt and black pepper.

Tip Can be made 1 day in advance; cover and chill.

 4   10 mins   Up to 3 days   **GF**

Tomato, Feta, and Crushed Almond Salad

This is my take on the classic Greek salad, refreshing and full of flavor. As this salad doesn't have tender greens, it's a good one to make in advance and keep in the fridge. Perfect for a picnic in the sun or an easy lunch to take to work.

7 oz feta (see note on page 16)
1 Tbsp chopped fresh oregano
1 Tbsp chopped fresh parsley
2 Tbsp olive oil
1 large green pepper, seeded, sliced into ¾-inch pieces
1 small red onion, very thinly sliced
1 baby cucumber, quartered lengthwise, then chopped
1 pint mixed grape tomatoes, halved
¼ cup pitted kalamata olives, halved
1 Tbsp chopped fresh mint
2 Tbsp balsamic or red wine vinegar
salt and black pepper

To serve
zest of 1 lemon
4 Tbsp almonds, toasted and crushed

1 Break the feta into chunks in a bowl, then add the oregano, parsley, and 1 tablespoon of the olive oil. Season with a small pinch of salt and black pepper, then gently turn the feta to coat in the herby oil.

2 Heat the remaining oil in a frying pan over medium-high heat, add the green pepper, and cook for about 8 minutes, until slightly softened and just starting to color. Remove the pan from the heat and use a slotted spoon or tongs to lift out the pepper. Set aside to cool for 5–10 minutes, reserving the oil.

3 In another bowl, mix the onion, cucumber, tomatoes, olives, mint, vinegar, and a generous pinch of salt. Gently fold in the green pepper. Serve the salad on a serving plate or divided into bowls, topped with the feta, lemon zest, and almonds and drizzled with the reserved oil.

Tips More bulk? Add roasted chickpeas or crispy tofu.

Making ahead? Sprinkle with a few fresh mint leaves just before serving.

 6 10 mins 10 mins Up to 5 days Up to 1 month   **GF**

Harissa Eggplant Kebabs with Zing Zing Grain Salad

A summery salad with barbecue vibes, this is crunchy, sweet, and bursting with big flavors and textures from tomatoes, cucumber, fresh herbs, sumac, lemon, and pomegranate. The hero, though, is the charred eggplant pieces, which are brushed with a spicy and sweet harissa and maple glaze and cooked until meltingly soft and sticky.

3 medium eggplants (or 2 large)
1 red onion, finely sliced
2 lemons
1 tsp ground sumac
3 tsp maple syrup
2 Tbsp harissa paste
1¼ cups bulgur wheat
1½ cups cherry tomatoes, halved
1 cucumber, cut into ⅜-inch cubes
5 oz pomegranate seeds
handful of fresh herbs (I used parsley and mint), roughly chopped
3 Tbsp olive oil
salt and black pepper
2 Tbsp toasted sesame seeds, to serve

1 Preheat the broiler to high. Cut the eggplant into large chunks—about 1½-inch pieces. Line a baking sheet with foil, spread out the eggplant pieces, and broil for 10–15 minutes, until charred.

2 Meanwhile, put the onion slices in the bottom of a large bowl. Add the zest and juice of 1 lemon, the sumac, 1 teaspoon of the maple syrup, and a big pinch of salt. Use your hands to scrunch everything together and then set aside so the onion can lightly pickle.

3 Mix the harissa with 3–4 tablespoons of water so it emulsifies into a sauce. Add the remaining maple syrup, season with salt and black pepper, and mix well.

4 Remove the eggplant from the oven and increase the heat to 425°F. Carefully slide the eggplant chunks onto skewers, lay them on the baking sheet, and either brush or spoon over the harissa mixture. Cover with foil and cook for 10–15 minutes, until very soft, removing the foil for the last 5 minutes so they become sticky.

5 While they cook, bring a saucepan of salted water to a boil, add the bulgur wheat, and cook according to the package instructions. Add the remaining ingredients for the salad to the large bowl with the pickled onion.

6 Drain and rinse the bulgur wheat in cold water, then add to the salad bowl and toss together. Taste, and season with salt and black pepper. Cut the remaining lemon into wedges. Spoon the salad into bowls, top with the skewers, scatter with sesame seeds, and serve with lemon wedges on the side.

Tips If you're cooking for friends in the summer, cook the eggplant on the grill outside!

The salad will keep for up to 3 days in the fridge.

 4
 20 mins
 20–30 mins
 Up to 3 days
 Up to 1 month

Charred Eggplant and Peanut Stew

My good friend Rachel Ama makes the most delicious sweet potato West African stew, and I took inspiration from it to make this charred and smoky eggplant version. Rich, spicy, creamy, salty, sharp, and sweet, it has everything going on!

1–2 medium eggplants, chopped into 1-inch pieces
4 Tbsp peanut oil, plus more if needed
1 onion, quartered
2 garlic cloves
1-inch piece fresh ginger
2 Tbsp chopped fresh cilantro stems, leaves reserved for a garnish
1 tsp ground coriander
1 tsp smoked paprika
½ tsp ground cumin
1 (14-oz) can chopped tomatoes
2 Tbsp tomato purée
½ tsp salt
¼ tsp black pepper
2 cups veg stock
½ cup peanut butter, either crunchy or smooth
rice or flatbreads, to serve

Pink onions
1 small red onion, sliced
1 Tbsp sugar
2 Tbsp red wine vinegar or apple cider vinegar

Tips Best served with fluffy rice or my Fragrant Flatbreads on page 206.

It may sound counterintuitive to soak the eggplants first, but it softens them up so you can squeeze out more of their liquid.

1 In a large bowl, soak the eggplant in warm water for 20 minutes, until soft.

2 Squeeze the eggplant to release its natural water. (It sounds crazy and a total waste of time, but it's better than adding salt to draw out the water—trust me!)

3 Heat 2 tablespoons of the oil in a frying pan over medium heat. Once warm, add the eggplant, flesh side down. Leave undisturbed for 3–4 minutes, until slightly charred. Stirring occasionally, cook for a further 5 minutes, until browned on all sides.

4 Meanwhile, in a food processor, blend the onion, garlic, ginger, cilantro stems, and spices to a paste consistency.

5 When the eggplant is cooked, transfer to a plate and wipe the pan clean. Heat the remaining 2 tablespoons oil in the frying pan over medium heat. Once warm, add the paste, stirring often, and cook for 5–7 minutes, adding more oil if the paste starts to stick.

6 Add the eggplant, chopped tomatoes, and tomato purée, and fry, stirring for about 1 minute. Season with the salt and black pepper. Add the stock and peanut butter and mix well. Simmer over medium heat for 15–20 minutes, stirring occasionally, until you have a thick sauce.

7 While the stew is cooking, put the sliced red onion in a small bowl. Add the sugar and vinegar and stir well. Set aside to pickle lightly.

8 Serve the stew with fluffy rice or flatbreads, topped with the pink onions and cilantro leaves.

 4   10 mins   30–40 mins   Up to 3 days   Up to 1 month   GF

Really Good Stuffed Peppers

Stuffed peppers may have a bit of a seventies vibe about them, but there's a reason they're still so popular—they're delicious! They're also very versatile. These have a strong taste of the Mediterranean from pine nuts, couscous, feta, olives, and golden raisins, rounded off with a harissa-tahini dressing. Just like flares and denim-on-denim, these never go out of fashion for long!

olive oil, for brushing
4 mixed peppers, or bell peppers, halved and seeded
1¼ cups couscous
2 garlic cloves, chopped
1–1¼ cups veg stock, boiling
16 pitted green olives, chopped
1 Tbsp drained capers
1¾ oz feta, crumbled, plus more for topping (see note on page 16)
¼ cup pine nuts, toasted
3 Tbsp golden raisins
zest of 1 lemon
2 Tbsp chopped fresh mint, plus more to serve
2 Tbsp chopped fresh parsley, plus more to serve
2 Tbsp chopped fresh dill, plus more to serve
salt and black pepper

Harissa-tahini dressing
1 Tbsp harissa paste
2 Tbsp tahini
1 Tbsp olive oil
1 tsp lemon juice

1   Preheat the oven to 350°F. Line a baking sheet with parchment paper and brush with olive oil.

2   Place the peppers on the baking sheet and cook in the oven for 15 minutes, until they are beginning to soften and are slightly charred around the edges.

3   Meanwhile, put the couscous and garlic in a heatproof bowl and pour in boiling stock to cover the couscous by ⅟₁₆–⅛ inch. Cover the bowl with a clean kitchen towel and set aside for 10–15 minutes, until the couscous is soft and fluffy.

4   Add the olives, capers, feta, pine nuts, raisins, lemon zest, and herbs; season to taste with salt and pepper and mix well.

5   Scoop the couscous mixture into the cooked peppers, topping with more feta. Bake for 10 minutes, until the peppers are soft and the filling lightly crisp and golden.

6   While they are cooking, make the harissa-tahini dressing by mixing the ingredients in a small bowl until smooth. If the sauce is too thick, add a splash of water to help loosen.

7   Remove the stuffed peppers from the oven and let them cool for a few minutes before serving. Drizzle the dressing on top and scatter with fresh herbs.

Tip These can be served cold. Prepare 1 day in advance, cover and keep chilled.

 4–8   10 mins   25 mins   Up to 3 days   Up to 1 month   **GF**

Spicy Red Pepper Dip with Crispy Harissa Ground "Meat"

This is my interpretation of an amazing dish—muhammara—a spicy Middle Eastern red pepper and walnut dip. It's very easy to pull together, especially if you use a jar of roasted peppers. I've topped mine with crispy harissa mince for a more complete meal, but if you leave it out it's perfect for parties, served with crudites or pita breads, or spread on the inside of sandwiches, like my Roasted Root Veg Sub Sandwiches on page 66.

2 Tbsp olive oil, plus more to drizzle
1 onion, finely diced
14 oz plant-based ground "meat"
1 garlic clove, minced
2 Tbsp harissa paste
handful of fresh parsley leaves,
  for garnish
handful of fresh dill leaves, for garnish
salt and black pepper

Muhammara
1 cup halved walnuts
1 (14-oz) jar roasted red peppers,
  drained, or 4–5 fresh red peppers,
  roasted (see Tip below)
4 Tbsp olive oil
juice of 1 lemon
1 tsp smoked paprika

To serve
1 lemon, cut into wedges
4–8 Fragrant Flatbreads (page 206)
  or rice

Tip If using fresh red peppers: preheat the oven to 400°F. Cut the peppers in half and remove the seeds and stems. Place on a parchment-lined baking sheet and roast for 20–25 minutes, until charred. Remove from oven and cool before removing the charred skin.

1 In a large frying pan, toast the walnuts for the muhammara for about 5 minutes over medium heat, occasionally shaking the pan, until the walnuts are fragrant and toasted. Remove from the pan and set aside.

2 Using the same frying pan, heat the 2 tablespoons of olive oil over medium heat, and fry the onion with a generous pinch of salt and black pepper, stirring often until very soft. Add the ground "meat" and turn the heat up slightly. Cook for 5–7 minutes, stirring occasionally, until the mixture is browned and crispy. Add the garlic and cook for a minute further, then spoon in the harissa and combine. Remove from heat and set aside.

3 Reserving 1 tablespoon for a garnish, pulse the toasted walnuts with the rest of the muhammara ingredients in a high-speed blender until it forms a smooth sauce. Taste and season with salt and pepper, then spread on a big platter using the back of a spoon.

4 Top the sauce with the crispy harissa mixture, scatter with the remaining walnuts, chopping them up a little if you want. Finish with fresh herbs, an extra drizzle of olive oil, and a pinch of black pepper. Serve with lemon wedges and flatbreads for scooping it all up, or with rice.

 4   10 mins   20 mins   Up to 5 days   Up to 1 month

Black Pepper Tofu Stir-Fry

Crispy, pan-fried tofu and stir-fried peppers are tossed together in a warm peppery glaze, fiery from the chiles and with an extra tongue-tingling kick from the black pepper. This stir-fry is a weeknight classic in my home, best served with fluffy white rice or noodles. You could also serve it as a side dish, as part of a feast.

Crispy tofu
1 (10-oz) block extra-firm tofu, cut into ¾-inch strips
1 Tbsp cornstarch
4 Tbsp vegetable oil

Black pepper sauce
3 Tbsp soy sauce or tamari
2 Tbsp black peppercorns, crushed (use a mortar and pestle or spice grinder)
1 Tbsp brown sugar
2 tsp hoisin sauce
2 tsp toasted sesame oil

Stir-fried peppers
1 Tbsp vegetable oil
2 red bell peppers, seeded and cut into ¾-inch squares
1 green bell pepper, seeded and cut into ¾-inch squares
1 shallot, thinly sliced
2 garlic cloves, finely chopped
1–2 spring onions, thinly sliced
1 Tbsp finely chopped fresh ginger
¼ tsp red pepper flakes
1 fresh red chile, thinly sliced

To serve
spring onions, thinly sliced
zest of 1 lime
rice or noodles

Tip If gluten is an issue for you, ensure you use tamari, a gluten-free version of soy sauce, and serve with rice or gluten-free noodles.

1 First, make the sauce. In a small bowl, whisk together the soy sauce, crushed black peppercorns, sugar, hoisin sauce, and sesame oil. Set aside.

2 To make the crispy tofu, blot the tofu dry, pressing to remove excess water. In a large bowl, toss the tofu with the cornstarch until evenly coated.

3 Heat the oil in a large non-stick frying pan over medium heat. Once hot, carefully drop in the tofu, separating the pieces so that they don't stick. Fry, undisturbed, for 2–3 minutes, until golden brown and lightly crispy on one side. Cook for a further 10–12 minutes, stirring occasionally, to fry all sides. Carefully tip the crispy tofu into a colander to drain.

4 Meanwhile, for the peppers, heat another large non-stick frying pan or wok over high heat. Add the oil, reduce the heat to medium-high, and add the peppers and shallot. Stir-fry for 4–5 minutes, until the peppers and shallot are soft. Add the garlic, spring onions, ginger, red pepper flakes, and chile and stir-fry for 45 seconds, until the garlic and ginger smell fragrant.

5 For the last minute of cooking, add the crispy tofu to the stir-fried peppers and pour in the sauce, then remove from the heat continuing to stir to coat everything evenly.

6 Serve hot, sprinkled with spring onions and lime zest, with noodles or rice.

 2–4 15 mins 15 mins Up to 3 days Up to 1 month

Sticky Eggplant and Peanut Salad

This is one of my all-time favorite ways to cook eggplant. The trick is to grill the eggplant without any oil for a really intense, smoky, charred flavor. Coated in a sweet, sticky maple-sriracha glaze, it's lip-smackingly good. With a zesty peanut butter dressing, fresh herbs, crunchy peanuts, spring onions, and sliced chile, this has so much going on! Serve with brown or white rice for a satisfying main course.

2 medium eggplants
2 Tbsp soy sauce or tamari
2 Tbsp maple syrup
1 Tbsp sriracha
2 Tbsp sesame oil

Sweet and spicy peanut sauce
2 Tbsp peanut butter, either smooth or
 crunchy
1 Tbsp sriracha
zest and juice of 1–2 limes
1 Tbsp maple syrup

To serve
⅓ cup peanuts, roughly chopped
4 Tbsp chopped fresh cilantro
4 Tbsp chopped fresh mint
3 spring onions, thinly sliced
1 fresh red chile, thinly sliced

1   Preheat the broiler as high as it will go. Slice the eggplants in half lengthwise and use a knife to cross-hatch the flesh. Arrange in a parchment-lined roasting pan and broil for 10 minutes or until charred. Remove the baking pan from the oven and turn the oven to 425°F.

2   Meanwhile, whisk together the soy sauce, maple syrup, sriracha, and sesame oil. Place the eggplant on a baking sheet lined with parchment paper and drizzle with the marinade. Cover with foil and roast for 20 minutes. Remove the foil cover and spoon any glaze in the tray over the eggplant, then roast for a further 8–10 minutes, uncovered, until very soft and sticky.

3   Whisk the ingredients for the sweet and spicy peanut sauce with enough water to make it a drizzleable consistency.

4   Place the eggplant on a large platter and drizzle with the sauce. Scatter over the peanuts, cilantro, mint, spring onions, and chile slices.

 2   15 mins   40 mins   Up to 5 days   Up to 1 month

Romesco Risotto

Smoky, charred roasted red peppers and walnut romesco sauce are stirred through risotto to produce this amazing deep red, richly flavored rice dish. If you have time, go ahead and roast your own peppers, but keeping some in a jar means this dish is a great cupboard standby. Serve with a big crunchy green salad.

1 (14-oz) jar roasted red peppers, or
  5 fresh red peppers, roasted
  (see Tip on page 102)
½ cup walnuts, toasted, plus more
  to serve
5 cups veg stock, warmed
2 Tbsp olive oil, plus more to serve
1 onion, finely chopped
2 garlic cloves, minced
1 Tbsp tomato purée
1 tsp smoked paprika
1½ cups arborio rice
⅔ cup dry white wine
salt and black pepper

To serve
handful of chopped fresh parsley
  leaves
grated parmesan (see note on page 16)
zest of 1 lemon

1 Drain the red peppers, reserving the liquid, then blend half of the roasted peppers with the toasted walnuts and 3 Tbsp of the stock in a food processor. Season well with salt and black pepper. Add the reserved jar liquid to the remaining stock. Roughly chop the remaining red peppers.

2 Heat the olive oil in a large high-sided frying pan over medium heat. Add the onion with a big pinch of salt and fry for 5 minutes, until softened. Add the garlic, tomato purée, and smoked paprika. Cook for 2 minutes, then add the rice. Stir and cook until the rice starts to make popping sounds.

3 Pour in the wine and cook, stirring, until it has been absorbed by the rice. Turn the heat down and add the stock, a ladle at a time, stirring until it's all absorbed. Be patient, risotto is best made slowly! Once the stock is all absorbed, stir in the red pepper and walnut sauce. Taste and season with salt and pepper. If the rice is a still a bit chalky, add a splash of water and cook a little longer; the rice should be cooked through with a slight bite. Stir in the chopped red peppers in the final minute of cooking.

4 Spoon into bowls, top with chopped parsley, grated parmesan, a scattering of reserved toasted crushed walnuts, lemon zest, a drizzle of olive oil, and a sprinkle of pepper.

Tip Best served hot!

 4   10 mins   30 mins   1–3 days   Up to 1 month

Ratatouille Grain Bowl

A big hit of veg in one bowl, this is inspired by the classic Provençal dish, which I've made more substantial by serving on garlicky grains. As it cooks in the oven, all the veg flavors soften into each other, producing a comforting, rounded dish with a subtle warm-cool contrasting mustard crème fraîche drizzled on top.

2 medium eggplants
2 red bell peppers
2 red onions
1 garlic head
4 Tbsp olive oil, plus more to drizzle
1 pint cherry tomatoes
1 tsp dried oregano
1½ cups freekeh or barley (or two 7-oz packages cooked mixed grains)
juice of 1 lemon
handful of fresh parsley, finely chopped
½ cup crème fraîche (see note on page 16)
1 tsp Dijon mustard
salt and black pepper

To serve
4 Tbsp roughly chopped toasted pine nuts
2 Tbsp torn fresh basil leaves

1   Preheat the oven to 400°F.

2   Roughly chop the eggplants into 1¼-inch pieces. Cut the tops off the peppers, remove the seeds, then cut into 1¼-inch pieces. Peel the red onions and cut into wedges. Add the prepped veg to a large roasting pan and snuggle in the whole garlic. Drizzle with 2 tablespoons of the olive oil, season well with salt and black pepper, and roast for 20 minutes.

3   Add the tomatoes and dried oregano and roast for a further 20 minutes, until everything is cooked through and soft.

4   Meanwhile, if you're using raw grains, rinse them well and cook in boiling water according to package instructions. Drain, rinse, and tip into a bowl. If you're using precooked grains, run under hot water for 10 seconds, drain well, and tip into a bowl. Add the lemon juice, remaining olive oil, and the parsley, and season well.

5   In a small bowl, mix the crème fraîche with the mustard and season well. Squeeze the garlic (it should be soft and golden brown) into the grains and give it a good stir.

6   To assemble, spoon the grains into bowls (or onto a big platter) and top with the roasted veggies. Drizzle with the mustard crème fraîche and finish with the pine nuts and basil leaves. Add a sprinkle of black pepper and a drizzle of olive oil.

 4–8   15 mins   40 mins   Up to 5 days   Up to 1 month

4– Gourds & Legumes

Pumpkin
Squash
Cucumber
Tofu
Chickpeas
Beans

Fresh Cucumber and Apple Salad

Magic happens when you combine cool cucumbers and crunchy apples. This is a perfect side dish for summer picnics and barbecues. It's addictively good and takes just minutes to make.

⅓ cup toasted pistachios, crushed
2 Tbsp white wine vinegar
1 tsp maple syrup
3 Tbsp extra-virgin olive oil
1 large cucumber, halved lengthwise, then halved crossways, then cut into ⅜-inch pieces
1 Granny Smith apple, cored and cut into thin slices
3 small radishes, thinly sliced
4 oz feta, roughly crumbled (see note on page 16)
¾ cup fresh basil leaves
2 Tbsp freshly torn mint
salt and black pepper

1   Put most of the pistachios (reserving some to garnish) in a food processor. Add the vinegar, maple syrup, and oil, and pulse for a few seconds until slightly smooth. Season to taste with salt and black pepper.

2   Combine the remaining salad ingredients in a serving bowl. Pour the pistachio dressing over the top and gently fold in. Sprinkle with the remaining pistachios and season with more salt and black pepper.

Tip This can be prepared 1 day in advance, but leave out the herbs and pistachios until just before serving.

 4
 5 mins
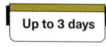 Up to 3 days

GF

Gourds & Legumes

Crisp Cucumber Salsa

With cool cucumber and spicy chile, this salsa has a surprisingly zingy crunch. It's the perfect accompaniment to any meal, especially my Pulled Mushroom Tacos (page 179), Smoky Lentil and Broccoli Stem Tacos (page 142), or Loaded Nachos (page 19).

2 baby cucumbers, quartered
  lengthwise, then thinly sliced
½ red onion, finely chopped
zest and juice of 1 lime
2 Tbsp chopped fresh mint
2 Tbsp chopped fresh cilantro
½ fresh red or green chile, seeded,
  finely chopped
generous pinch of salt
¼ tsp black pepper

In a bowl, combine the cucumbers, red onion, lime juice and zest, mint, cilantro, and chile. Season with salt and black pepper and leave for about 10 minutes before serving. This will allow the flavors to blend and will also remove some of the liquid from the cucumber, providing a less watery crunch.

Tips Make 1 day in advance if needed; keep for 3 days in the fridge in a sealed container.

You may want more chile, or less, depending on the chile heat and how spicy you like it.

 8 15 mins Up to 3 days **GF**

Creamy Zucchini and Lemon Linguine

This easy pasta dish is a must-make for using up zucchini or yellow summer squash. Flavors of olive oil, shallots, and garlic are held together by a lip-smackingly creamy cashew sauce, all lifted by a final squeeze of lemon. Grating zucchini means you can use the entire thing—yes, even the stalk. It all cooks down in the pan since it's mainly water. A fantastic summertime pasta dish that can be eaten warm or cold.

2 large zucchini or yellow summer squash
2 Tbsp olive oil
1 shallot or ½ small onion, thinly sliced
4 garlic cloves, finely grated
12 oz linguine or any long pasta
⅓ cup raw cashews, soaked in hot water for 20–30 minutes, then rinsed
zest and juice of 1 lemon
1 cup grated parmesan, plus more to serve (see note on page 16)
1 tsp cornstarch
2 Tbsp extra-virgin olive oil
1 Tbsp drained capers or pitted green olives
3 Tbsp chopped fresh basil
3 Tbsp chopped fresh mint
salt and black pepper

1   Using the large holes of a box grater, grate the zucchini into a bowl. Use your hands to squeeze out any excess liquid, then place the zucchini on a clean kitchen towel. Wrap the kitchen towel around the zucchini and squeeze the remaining liquid out over the sink.

2   Heat the olive oil in a large frying pan over medium heat and cook the shallot for 8–10 minutes, stirring occasionally, until soft. Stir in half of the garlic and cook for 2–3 minutes, until lightly browned. Add the grated zucchini and increase the heat to medium-high. Season with salt and black pepper and cook for 3–5 minutes, stirring often, until the zucchini begins to soften. Remove from the heat.

3   Meanwhile, bring a large pan of salted water to a boil, add the pasta, and cook according to the package instructions.

4   In a blender, purée the soaked cashews, the remaining garlic, lemon juice, parmesan, cornstarch, extra-virgin olive oil, and 4 tablespoons of the pasta cooking water until smooth and creamy; you may need to scrape the sides down halfway through. Season with salt and black pepper.

5   Drain the pasta and immediately transfer to the pan with the zucchini, and place pan over low heat. Pour half the cashew sauce over the pasta, stirring until the sauce coats the pasta. Toss in the capers, lemon zest, and the basil and mint, reserving a little for a garnish.

6   Serve the pasta in bowls, topped with the remaining sauce, a sprinkle of grated parmesan, and the rest of the basil and mint.

Tip Use gluten-free pasta if you prefer.

 4
 15 mins
 15–20 mins
 Up to 3 days
 Up to 1 month

Roasted Squash and Eggplant with Tahini Yogurt and Toasted Seeds

In this warm eggplant and squash salad, subtle heat from the harissa dressing is cooled down by creamy tahini yogurt sauce. It's so versatile: serve as a starter with pita or flatbreads, or as a main course with rice or pasta. Go ahead and switch up the type of squash: zucchini or butternut squash will also work well. For extra sweetness, feel free to throw in a couple of onions peeled and sliced into wedges, too, which will caramelize and soften beautifully in the oven.

1¼ lb yellow summer squash, cut into ¾-inch pieces
1 eggplant, cut into ⅜-inch pieces
4 garlic cloves: 2 lightly crushed, 2 thinly sliced
3 fresh thyme sprigs
zest and juice of 1 lemon
6 Tbsp extra-virgin olive oil
1 Tbsp tahini
½ cup yogurt (I use coconut)
2 Tbsp pine nuts
2 Tbsp sunflower seeds
1 Tbsp sesame seeds
1 tsp harissa paste
2 Tbsp chopped fresh dill
salt and black pepper
toasted pita bread, to serve (optional)

1 Preheat the oven to 350°F.

2 In a roasting pan, mix the squash, eggplant, crushed garlic, thyme sprigs, lemon zest, 3 tablespoons of the olive oil, and a generous pinch of salt until everything is coated in the oil. Roast for about 1½ hours, turning everything over every 30 minutes or so, until the veg is softened and starting to get a little crunchy on the surface. Set aside to cool while you make the rest of the recipe.

3 In a small bowl, whisk the tahini and yogurt with the lemon juice and a splash of water until smooth and creamy. Season with salt and black pepper.

4 In a frying pan over medium-low heat, toast the pine nuts and sunflower and sesame seeds for about 3 minutes, shaking the pan occasionally, until lightly brown.

5 In another small bowl, whisk together the remaining 3 tablespoons of olive oil, the harissa, thinly sliced garlic, and the toasted seed mixture. Season with salt and black pepper.

6 Spread the tahini yogurt sauce across a serving platter. Top with the veg, the seed mixture, and fresh dill. Serve warm, with toasted pita if you like.

Tip This salad is best served hot.

 4   15 mins   1½ hours   Up to 3 days   Up to 1 month   **GF**

Roast Dinner Tart

This incredible tart has all your favorite elements of a roast dinner. It's the perfect alternative Sunday lunch or festive meal –just don't forget the gravy!

1 large beet
½ butternut squash
4 medium carrots
3 medium parsnips
3 Tbsp olive oil
1 recipe Best Roasted Potatoes
  (page 33)
1 recipe Buttery Herb Stuffing
  (page 74)
2 Tbsp nutritional yeast
1 tsp ground cinnamon
1 tsp grated nutmeg
1 sheet gluten-free puff pastry
oat milk, for brushing
4 oz Brussels sprouts, halved
6 Tbsp cranberry sauce
salt and black pepper
gravy, to serve

Crispy sage
8–10 sage leaves
3 Tbsp olive oil

1 Preheat the oven to 475°F.

2 Wrap the beet in foil and put on one side of a baking pan. Place the squash next to it, cut side down. Roast for up to 1 hour (depending on size), until the beet is totally soft. If the squash cooks more quickly, remove it from the oven and let the beet keep cooking.

3 Slice the carrots and parsnips in half lengthwise and put in roasting pan. Drizzle with 1 Tbsp olive oil, add a pinch of salt, and roast for 30 minutes, until soft and charred. Remove from the oven but leave oven on.

4 Make the potatoes following the recipe.

5 Make the stuffing following the recipe.

6 Scoop the seeds from the squash and set aside (you can rinse them and toast them for a snack). In a blender, purée the squash with the nutritional yeast, cinnamon, and nutmeg. Season well.

7 Slip the skin off the beet and slice into wedges.

8 Cut the sheet of puff pastry into 4 rectangles. Lightly score a border, ¾ inch from the edge. Brush with oat milk, then bake for 20–30 minutes until golden and risen; use a spoon to push the middle down.

9 Meanwhile, heat the remaining olive oil in a large frying pan over medium heat, add the sprouts with a pinch of salt, and fry for 5 minutes. Add a big splash of water and cook for a further 5 minutes, until tender. Set aside.

10 Make the crispy sage. Heat the oil in a small frying pan over high heat. Once hot, fry the sage for 2 minutes until crispy. Set aside to drain on kitchen paper.

11 Spoon the butternut squash purée onto each pastry rectangle, then crumble over the stuffing. Top with the carrots, parsnips, beet, and roasted potatoes. Scatter over the sprouts, then spoon over a little cranberry sauce. Finish with the crispy sage leaves and serve with lots of gravy.

 4
 30 mins
1 hour 20– 1 hour 30 mins
 Up to 1 week
 Up to 1 month
GF

Curried Pumpkin and Chickpeas

A simple, warm, and inviting autumn dish, roasted pumpkin and spiced chickpeas are heaped onto a creamy and tangy yogurt sauce. It's elevated with toasted coconut flakes, crispy onions, and fresh cilantro, which add texture and extra flavor. Serve with rice and my Fragrant Flatbreads (page 206) to make the ultimate feast!

1 pumpkin (approx. 2 lb)

3 Tbsp olive oil

2 (14-oz) cans chickpeas, drained and rinsed (reserve the aquafaba to make my meringues on page 228)

1 Tbsp cumin seeds

1–2 tsp chili powder

scant 1 cup coconut yogurt or other thick yogurt

2 limes

small handful of fresh cilantro, roughly chopped

small handful of fresh mint, roughly chopped

⅓ cup crispy onions

½ cup shredded coconut, toasted

salt and black pepper

1   Preheat the oven to 425°F.

2   Cut the pumpkin in half, remove the seeds, then cut into wedges. Place the wedges flesh side up on a large baking sheet. Drizzle with 2 tablespoons of the olive oil, season with salt and black pepper, and roast for 30 minutes.

3   Meanwhile, on another baking sheet, toss the chickpeas with the remaining olive oil, cumin seeds, chili powder, and a generous pinch of salt. Once the pumpkin has been roasting for about 15 minutes, put the chickpeas in the oven and cook for 15 minutes, until the pumpkin and chickpeas are golden brown and crispy.

4   Meanwhile, in a small bowl, mix the yogurt with the zest and juice of 1 lime and half of the fresh herbs. Season with salt and pepper and spread across a large platter.

5   Top with the roasted chickpeas, then the cooked pumpkin wedges. Scatter over the crispy onions, toasted coconut, and remaining cilantro and mint. Serve with lime wedges.

Tips Try swapping the pumpkin for butternut squash, delicata squash, or sweet potato.

The pumpkin seeds can be toasted and enjoyed later as a snack.

 4–8   10 mins   30 mins   Up to 5 days   Up to 1 month

Grilled Zucchini and Miso-Almond "Ricotta" Involtini

This is an easy yet impressive dish that is great for entertaining. Strips of grilled zucchini are stuffed with creamy almond "ricotta," rolled up, and baked in a flavorful sea of tomato sauce. My almond "ricotta" is super-easy to make and comes together in minutes.

2 large zucchini
2 Tbsp olive oil
2 cups prepared tomato sauce (try my Simplest Tomato Sauce, page 87)
4 fresh thyme sprigs
salt and black pepper

To serve
red pepper flakes
chopped fresh basil
grated parmesan (see note on page 16)

Almond "ricotta"
1 cup sliced almonds, soaked in hot water for 20–30 minutes, then rinsed and drained
¼ cup hot water
zest and juice of ½ lemon
2 tsp extra-virgin olive oil
2 tsp white miso
2 Tbsp nutritional yeast
2 garlic cloves, finely grated
3 Tbsp chopped fresh basil
2 Tbps chopped fresh parsley

1   First, make the almond "ricotta." In a high-speed blender, purée the almonds, hot water, lemon juice and zest, olive oil, miso, nutritional yeast, and garlic until smooth but still slightly textured. If it seems a little thick, add a little more hot water. Stir in the basil and parsley, then chill in the fridge.

2   Using a mandolin slicer or sharp knife, slice the zucchini lengthwise, including the stems, into thin strips (about ⅛ inch thick). Put the strips in a bowl and toss with the olive oil, salt, and pepper.

3   Preheat the broiler to medium-high. Place a wire rack inside a large roasting pan and arrange the zucchini slices on the rack. Broil for 5–8 minutes until lightly charred, then flip them over and cook until charred on the other side. Remove from the rack and set aside.

4   Set the oven to 375°F.

5   Pour the tomato sauce into a 9-inch ovenproof dish. Set up an assembly line with a cutting board, the zucchini slices, and the almond "ricotta." Lay one zucchini slice on the cutting board and place 1 tablespoon of the almond "ricotta" at the wider end. Carefully and gently roll it up, so that no ricotta squeezes out the sides. Carefully place the roll in the tomato sauce. Repeat until you have rolled all the zucchini.

6   Place the thyme sprigs on top of the involtini. Cover loosely with foil, to allow steam to escape, and bake for 15–20 minutes, until heated through.

7   Serve hot, sprinkled with red pepper flakes, chopped basil, and grated parmesan.

Tip The almond "ricotta" can be made 2 days in advance.

 4   20–30 mins   25–35 mins   Up to 3 days   Up to 1 month   GF

Tofu Butter "Chicken"

A fan favorite, this is one of my most popular dishes with over 4 million views on my social media channels! Pressing the tofu removes excess water, and coating it with cornstarch gives it a thin, crunchy exterior when it's baked until golden in the oven. Paired with a vibrant, creamy sauce, it's winner winner (tofu) chicken dinner!

Tofu
1 (1-lb) block extra-firm tofu
2 Tbsp cornstarch

Sauce
1 large onion, finely chopped
3 garlic cloves, thinly sliced
2 Tbsp grated fresh ginger
1 Tbsp garam masala
1 tsp cumin seeds or ground cumin
1 tsp coriander seeds or ground coriander
½ tsp ground turmeric
½ tsp ground cinnamon
½ tsp chili powder
3 Tbsp butter (see note on page 16) or olive oil
pinch of salt and black pepper
3 Tbsp tomato purée
1 (14-oz) can full-fat coconut milk

To serve
toasted coconut flakes
yogurt (I use coconut)
fresh cilantro
fluffy basmati rice
Fragrant Flatbreads (page 206)

1 Cut the tofu in half. Wrap each half in a clean kitchen towel. Stack something heavy on top, such as a heavy pot, and leave for 10–15 minutes to press the liquid from the tofu.

2 Meanwhile, preheat the oven to 400°F. Line a baking sheet with parchment paper.

3 Tear the tofu into smaller pieces to resemble pieces of chicken. Place the tofu in a mixing bowl with the cornstarch and gently toss to coat the tofu pieces. Spread out the tofu pieces on the baking sheet and bake for 20–25 minutes, until the edges start to brown, flipping halfway through.

4 Meanwhile, in a food processor, process the onion, garlic, and ginger to a paste. In a large frying pan over medium heat, toast the spices for 1–2 minutes until fragrant, then stir in the paste and cook for 1 minute. Add the butter, salt, and pepper and stir, cooking for 3–4 minutes until the onion mixture is soft. Add the tomato purée and cook for 1 minute. Pour in the coconut milk, stir to combine, and simmer for 10 minutes.

5 When the tofu is brown and crispy, take the sauce off the heat and add the baked tofu. Serve with toasted coconut flakes, yogurt, fresh cilantro, fluffy rice, and flatbreads.

Tips Some might say that the leftovers are better the next day.

More bulk? Add roasted chickpeas and a handful of leafy greens.

Fun fact It's said that in Delhi in the early 20th century, butter chicken was a way to use up leftover chicken—a perfect fit for a cookbook that's all about cooking the food you already have.

 4 20 mins 20–25 mins 2–3 days Up to 3 months **GF**

Sticky, Spicy Ginger and Garlic Tofu

This is one of my go-to dishes for midweek meals. The trick here is, once the sauce is poured on the crispy tofu, turn the heat off, stir to coat the tofu, and serve immediately. Use the leftover sauce from the pan as an additional glaze for the noodles.

Sauce
¼ cup soy sauce or tamari
2 Tbsp coconut sugar or light brown sugar
1 Tbsp hot sauce
zest and juice of ½ lime
1 Tbsp vegetable oil
pinch of salt
¼ tsp black pepper

Spicy tofu
1 lb firm tofu, lightly crumbled
2 Tbsp cornstarch
3 Tbsp vegetable oil
1 small piece fresh ginger, not peeled, grated
2 garlic cloves, finely chopped

To serve
7 oz ramen noodles, prepared according to package instructions
1 Tbsp sesame seeds, lightly toasted
1–2 spring onions, thinly sliced
2 Tbsp chopped fresh cilantro
zest of ½ lime
lime wedges

Tips Replace the tofu with chickpeas, beans, tempeh, or mushrooms.

Use any style of Asian noodle you like: gluten-free works well. Or serve with rice.

I like to use up leftover condiments I have in my fridge—hot sauces, hot pepper jellies, anything pickled—as extra toppings.

1 First, prepare the sauce: in a bowl, whisk all the ingredients together until smooth and pourable. Set aside.

2 For the spicy tofu, toss the tofu and cornstarch in a bowl until evenly coated. Heat the oil in a large non-stick pan over medium heat. Once hot, carefully add the tofu and fry for 6–8 minutes, stirring often, until crispy and golden brown. Add the ginger and garlic and stir for 1–2 minutes until lightly brown.

3 Carefully pour the sauce over the tofu, remove from the heat, and stir. The sauce should bubble and sizzle.

4 Serve the noodles in bowls, add the spicy tofu, and top with toasted sesame seeds, spring onions, cilantro, lime zest, and a lime wedge.

 4 10 mins 10 mins 1–2 days   Up to 1 month

Killer Tofu "Ground Beef"

This is the most popular dish on my social media channels. Use this baked and seasoned tofu in any dishes traditionally prepared with ground beef. It's perfect for nachos (page 19), tacos, shepherd's pie, chili, and so much more. It's super-easy to prepare, the oven does all the hard work for you, and, best of all, it's made with just a few basic ingredients you probably already have in your cupboard.

1 (1-lb) block extra-firm tofu
3 Tbsp soy sauce or tamari
1 tsp garlic powder
1 tsp paprika
1 tsp chili powder
1 garlic clove, grated
1 tsp cornstarch
1 tsp tomato purée
2 Tbsp nutritional yeast
1 Tbsp olive oil

1 Preheat the oven to 400°F. Line a baking sheet with parchment paper.

2 Wrap the tofu in a clean kitchen towel or kitchen paper and lightly pat for about 2 minutes to remove some of the excess liquid.

3 Add the remaining ingredients (except the oil) to a large bowl and mix.

4 Into the same bowl, squeeze the pressed tofu between your hands to create a crumbly texture. Mix well to coat the tofu thoroughly.

5 Spread the tofu in an even layer on the baking sheet. Drizzle the oil over the tofu and bake for 20 minutes, tossing halfway through so it crisps up all over.

 4
 5 mins
 20 mins
 2–3 days
 Up to 3 months

Chickpea "Tuna" Salad

I'm happy to admit that I'm a tiny bit competitive, and so if my wife makes something in the kitchen, I'll usually try to make it better! This recipe is based on a lunch she cooked for us one day–but it's my improved version! Mashed chickpeas are given a distinctly fish-like flavor from the nori, and it has loads of texture from all the crunchy veg and seeds. It's a great protein-packed topping for baked potatoes or to use in sandwiches.

1 (14-oz) can chickpeas, drained and rinsed (reserve aquafaba for another recipe)
3 Tbsp mayonnaise
zest and juice of 1 lemon
½ red onion, finely chopped
1 red bell pepper, seeded and diced
2 celery stalks, thinly sliced, including the leaves
2 Tbsp drained capers
3 Tbsp toasted sunflower or pumpkin seeds
2 Tbsp chopped fresh dill
1 nori sheet, thinly sliced or flaked
pinch of salt
¼ tsp black pepper

1   Put the chickpeas in a bowl and crush, using the back of a fork or a potato masher, until the chickpeas are roughly mashed.

2   Add the mayo, lemon juice and zest, red onion, red pepper, celery, capers, toasted seeds, dill, nori, salt, and black pepper. Mix to your desired consistency.

3   Serve chilled or at room temperature.

Tips Serve on toasted bread, in a wrap or sandwich, or on a baked potato.

For a gluten-free version, serve on romaine lettuce leaves with cherry tomatoes.

Optional extras: add corn, peas, edamame, grated carrot, chopped cherry tomatoes.

 4   10 mins   1–2 days   Up to 1 month   **GF**

Crispy Tofu Burger

Coated in breadcrumbs and shallow-fried until golden brown, this almost exactly resembles the textures of a crispy fish burger. Pile into a ciabatta bun with all your favorite toppings—and be generous with the burger sauce.

¾ cup all-purpose flour
⅔ cup oat milk
1 tsp smoked paprika
½ cup panko breadcrumbs or homemade breadcrumbs
2 Tbsp sesame seeds
10 oz firm tofu, sliced horizontally into 4 rectangles, around ¾ inch thick
vegetable oil, for frying

Burger sauce
4 Tbsp ketchup
4 Tbsp mayonnaise
1 Tbsp Dijon mustard or yellow mustard
juice of ½ lemon

To serve
4 ciabatta rolls
½ cucumber, cut into ⅜-inch slices
1–2 tomatoes, depending on their size, cut into ⅜-inch slices
1 iceberg lettuce, shredded

1 In a small bowl, make the burger sauce by combining everything together. Keep the sauce and the prepared veg to serve in the fridge to keep cool.

2 In a bowl, whisk the flour, oat milk, and smoked paprika to make a thick batter. Combine the breadcrumbs and sesame seeds in a separate shallow bowl. Dip each of the tofu rectangles first in the batter, then dredge in the sesame breadcrumbs to coat all over.

3 Pour the vegetable oil ⅛ inch up the sides of a heavy-bottomed frying pan over medium-high heat. Once the oil is shimmering—after 2–3 minutes—check readiness by dropping a few breadcrumbs into the oil. If they sizzle, it's ready to go! Gently lower the breaded tofu into the oil and cook for 2–3 minutes on each side, until golden and crispy. Remove with a slotted spoon and drain on a wire rack or plate lined with paper towels. You may need to do this in 2 batches.

4 Slice the ciabatta rolls in half, lightly toast, and slather one side with the burger sauce. Layer up the crispy tofu, with slices of cucumber and tomato and the shredded lettuce. Eat as soon as possible.

Tip Best served hot!

 4
 15 mins
 15 mins
 Up to 1 month

Peas and Beans Fritters

These super-green fritters are so quick and easy to make and are one of my favorite ways to enjoy peas and beans. Serve as an appetizer or side, or make them smaller for tasty canapés.

1 (14-oz) package frozen peas
1 (14-oz) can white beans, such as cannellini or butter beans, drained and rinsed
5 Tbsp chickpea flour
2 garlic cloves, finely chopped
2 spring onions, thinly sliced
zest and juice of 1 lemon, plus more to serve (optional)
2 Tbsp chopped fresh mint
2 Tbsp chopped fresh parsley
2 Tbsp chopped fresh dill
olive oil or vegetable oil, for frying
salt and black pepper
yogurt (I use coconut or soy), to serve

1 Put the frozen peas in a large bowl, cover with boiling water, and leave for about 1 minute to defrost. Drain and set aside.

2 In a food processor, pulse the white beans with half of the peas to a roughly mashed texture, then add to the bowl with the remaining peas. Add the flour, garlic, spring onions, lemon juice and zest, and the herbs (reserving a few to garnish if you wish). Season with a generous pinch of salt and black pepper and mix well.

3 Place a large non-stick frying pan over medium heat and pour in enough oil to cover the bottom. Add a few tablespoons of the mixture to make each fritter and fry for about 3 minutes on each side, carefully flipping, until the edges are crispy. Remove with a slotted spoon and drain on a wire rack or plate lined with kitchen paper. You may need to do this in 2 batches.

4 Serve the fritters warm or at room temperature, with yogurt; if you wish, sprinkle with lemon juice and zest and fresh herbs.

Tip Any leftovers are great for breakfast or lunch the next day with a dollop of yogurt or sour cream (see page 19 for Sour Cream).

 6   10 mins   20 mins   Up to 3 days   Up to 1 month   **GF**

Smoked Pea Carbonara

I'm a bit obsessed with this dish! Tofu is used in two ways: for the crispy "pancetta" and to produce the luxurious creamy sauce. It's all brought together with pops of color and sweetness from the peas.

¾ cup frozen peas
3½ oz spaghetti
1 (7-oz) block smoked extra-firm tofu, pressed to remove water, then cut into small cubes
1 Tbsp cornstarch
½ tsp smoked paprika
2 Tbsp olive oil
2 garlic cloves, minced
grated parmesan, to serve (see note on page 16)

The sauce
10 oz silken tofu
4 Tbsp oat milk
1 tsp Dijon mustard
zest and juice of 1 lemon
1 Tbsp nutritional yeast
1 Tbsp white miso paste
⅛ tsp black pepper

1 Bring a large pan of salted water to a boil. Meanwhile, make the sauce by blending all the ingredients in a high-speed blender and set aside.

2 Pour the peas into a heatproof bowl, cover with boiling water, leave for 2 minutes, then drain and set aside.

3 Add the spaghetti to the pan of boiling water and cook for 1 minute less than package instructions.

4 While the spaghetti cooks, in a bowl lightly toss the cubed tofu, cornstarch, and smoked paprika until evenly coated. Heat the olive oil in a large frying pan over high heat and once warm, fry the cubed smoked tofu, stirring occasionally, for 8–10 minutes until crispy and brown. Add the garlic and cook for 30 seconds.

5 When the pasta is almost ready, pour the sauce into the frying pan with the tofu, stirring frequently, and cook until bubbling. Use tongs to transfer the pasta from the saucepan into the large frying pan with the sauce. Add the peas and toss everything well.

6 Serve in bowls, topped with black pepper and parmesan.

Tip Make your own smoked tofu by marinating a block of tofu with 1 tablespoon soy sauce or tamari, 2 teaspoons liquid smoke, 1 teaspoon smoked paprika, and 1 teaspoon maple syrup overnight in a small container. Make sure that the tofu is well coated with the sauce.

 4
 10 mins
 15 mins
 Up to 5 days
 Up to 1 month

Lentil Pappa Pomodoro

This dish came about as a result of a happy accident in my kitchen. I had some leftover lentil ragù and I didn't want to cook pasta, so I added some bread to it—and hey presto! Satisfying, grounded, and delicious, the bread adds extra bulk to the rich tomato soup.

2 Tbsp olive oil, plus more to drizzle
1 onion, finely chopped
2 garlic cloves, finely sliced
1 tsp dried oregano
½ tsp fennel seeds
1 cup cooked de Puy lentils
2 Tbsp tomato purée
2 (14-oz) cans plum tomatoes
2 generous cups veg stock
pinch of sugar (optional)
½ loaf crusty bread, torn
salt and black pepper
basil leaves, to serve

1   Heat 1 Tbsp of olive oil in a saucepan over medium heat. Add the onion and a big pinch of salt and fry, stirring often, for 5–8 minutes, until softened. Add the garlic, oregano, fennel seeds, and lentils, and cook for 2 minutes. Stir in the tomato purée and cook for a further 1–2 minutes. Add the tomatoes and stock, stirring to combine. Turn the heat down to a simmer and cook for 20–25 minutes, until slightly thickened and fragrant. Taste and season with salt and pepper and a pinch of sugar if it needs it.

2   Preheat the oven to 400°F.

3   While the sauce is cooking, put the torn crusty bread on a baking sheet, drizzle with the remaining olive oil, and toss together. Bake for 5–7 minutes, until lightly crispy and golden brown.

4   Add the crusty bread to the tomato mixture and cook for 3–5 minutes, stirring often. If it looks a little thick, add a splash of water to help loosen it. Spoon into bowls, drizzle with olive oil, and scatter with basil leaves. Finish with a sprinkle of black pepper.

Tip   You can use chickpeas in place of the lentils.

 6   5 mins   30–45 mins   Up to 5 days   Up to 1 month

No-Bake Pumpkin Pie in a Jar

What could be better than getting a mini pumpkin pie in a jar all to yourself?! These individual, no-oven-required, make-ahead desserts are made up of layers of crunchy pecan crust, spiced pumpkin, and silky coconut cream. This recipe makes four, but it easily doubles, triples, or quadruples. You can make them ahead and leave in the fridge to chill.

Coconut cream
6 oz full-fat coconut cream, at room temperature
3 Tbsp cream cheese (see note on page 16)
½ tsp vanilla extract
1 Tbsp maple syrup

Pecan crust
¾ cup pecans
½ cup Medjool dates, pits removed
⅓ cup almond flour
2 tsp light brown sugar
1 tsp ground cinnamon
generous pinch of salt

Pumpkin filling
1½ cups cooked pumpkin or butternut squash
2 Tbsp full-fat coconut cream
2 Tbsp maple syrup
2 Tbsp confectioners' sugar
1 tsp ground cinnamon
½ tsp ground nutmeg
½ tsp ground ginger
pinch of salt

1 First, make the coconut cream by whisking all the ingredients together until light and fluffy, then chill for 30 minutes.

2 To make the pecan crust, pulse the ingredients in a food processor to a light crumble consistency, then tip into a bowl.

3 To make the pumpkin filling, blend the ingredients in a food processor until smooth and creamy.

4 To assemble, you will need 4 small glass jars. Add a thin layer of the pecan crust to each jar, then a layer of the pumpkin filling and then the coconut cream. Repeat until you reach the top of the jar. Finish with a light dusting of the pecan crust.

5 Chill for at least 1–2 hours or overnight before serving.

 4   10 mins   Up to 7 days   Up to 1 month GF

5– Leafy Greens & Cruciferous

Cauliflower
Broccoli
Herbs

Smoky Lentil and Broccoli Stem Tacos

Meat-eaters and vegans alike will enjoy this budget-friendly take on tacos. A handful of surprisingly simple ingredients lends big flavors and "meaty" textures to the smoky lentil and broccoli stem taco filling.

2 Tbsp olive oil
½ red onion, thinly sliced
1 large broccoli stem, grated
1 (14-oz) can green lentils, drained and rinsed
2 garlic cloves, finely chopped
4 sun-dried tomatoes, roughly chopped
1 Tbsp tomato purée
1 Tbsp soy sauce or tamari
1 tsp smoked paprika
1 tsp ground cumin
1 Tbsp nutritional yeast
¼ tsp black pepper

To serve
8–12 corn or flour tortillas, warmed
Crisp Cucumber Salsa (page 114)
chopped fresh cilantro and basil
lime wedges

1 Heat the oil in a large frying pan over medium heat and cook the onion for 3–5 minutes, stirring occasionally, until soft. Add the grated broccoli stem, lentils, garlic, and sun-dried tomatoes and cook for 2–3 minutes, stirring occasionally.

2 Add all the remaining ingredients and cook for about 3 minutes, stirring frequently, until the mixture thickens and begins to stick to the pan. Stir in 1–2 tablespoons of water for the last minute of cooking. Remove from the heat and cover with a lid while you warm the tortillas.

3 To serve, spoon the lentil and broccoli mixture onto warm tortillas and top with salsa, cilantro, and basil, with lime wedges on the side.

Tips This is super-versatile: use as a substitute for the Killer Tofu "Ground Beef" in the nachos on page 19, or use in chili, burritos, or rice bowls.

If gluten is an issue for you, ensure you use tamari, a gluten-free version of soy sauce, and gluten-free corn tortillas.

 4
 10 mins
 10–15 mins
 Up to 3 days
 Up to 1 month

Broccoli Stem Fried Rice

Did you know that broccoli plants can grow nearly 3 feet high? What are we doing with all those stems?! Broccoli stems have a fantastic, subtly sweet flavor. You can eat them raw, sliced in a salad, or grate them into this quick and tasty midweek sir-fry, which has become one of my favorite ways to use up leftover broccoli stems.

¾ cup water or veg stock
⅔ cup white or brown rice, rinsed
1 Tbsp olive oil
1-inch piece fresh ginger, finely grated
4 garlic cloves, thinly sliced
10 oz shiitake mushrooms, sliced if large
1 large broccoli stem, grated
1 Tbsp butter (see note on page 16)
2 Tbsp soy sauce or tamari
1 tsp maple syrup
zest and juice of ½ lemon

To serve
⅔ cup thinly shredded red cabbage
½ carrot, cut into thin matchsticks
2 Tbsp finely chopped fresh cilantro
2 Tbsp finely chopped fresh chives
1–2 Tbsp toasted sesame seeds
½ tsp red pepper flakes

Tips Super-versatile: add chopped leftover veggies from your fridge.

Add protein: crispy tofu, roasted chickpeas, or plant-based "meat."

Use day-old cooked rice to make fried rice (another great way to waste less food)–but in this case, don't freeze.

If gluten is an issue for you, ensure you use tamari, a gluten-free version of soy sauce.

1 In a pan, bring the water to a boil. Add the rice, gently stir, reduce the heat, and simmer, uncovered, for 10–15 minutes or until the rice is cooked. (Brown rice will take 20–30 minutes to cook, and you may need to top up the pan with more boiling water.) Drain and set aside.

2 Meanwhile, add the oil to a non-stick frying pan over medium heat, stir in the ginger and garlic, and cook for 1 minute, until fragrant. Add the mushrooms and cook for 3–5 minutes, stirring occasionally, until the mushrooms are soft. Add the grated broccoli stem and cook for another 3–5 minutes, stirring often, until the mixture begins to stick to the pan.

3 Using a wooden spoon, push the veg to one side of the pan and melt the butter, then add the cooked rice and stir to combine everything. Add the soy sauce, maple syrup, and lemon juice and stir again, then leave to cook for 3–5 minutes without stirring, until the rice is slightly charred and begins to stick to the pan.

4 Serve the fried rice on a serving plate; top with shredded cabbage and carrot, chopped herbs, toasted sesame seeds, red pepper flakes, and lemon zest.

 4
 15 mins
 15–20 mins
 1 day
 Up to 1 month

Sticky Broccoli and Crispy Tofu

Crispy tofu is served with broccoli tossed in a sweet, spicy glaze. The key to crispy tofu is ensuring it's as dry as possible before it goes into the hot oil. You don't need takeout when you can make something more delicious in less time.

Crispy tofu
1 (10-oz) block extra-firm tofu
2 Tbsp cornstarch
4 Tbsp vegetable oil
salt and black pepper

Glazed broccoli
8 oz broccoli, cut into florets, stems
  sliced lengthwise
zest and juice of 1 lime
2 tsp soy sauce or tamari
2 tsp maple syrup or brown sugar
½ tsp red pepper flakes

To serve
rice or noodles
1–2 Tbsp crushed toasted peanuts

1   Wrap the tofu in a clean kitchen towel, cover with a weighted pan, and leave for 15-20 minutes. Blot the tofu dry, then cut into cubes.

2   In a large bowl, toss the tofu with the cornstarch until evenly coated.

3   Heat the oil in a large non-stick frying pan over medium-high heat. Once hot, carefully add the tofu—without crowding the pan—and fry, undisturbed, for 2–3 minutes until golden brown and crispy on one side. Cook for a further 5–7 minutes, stirring occasionally, to fry all sides. Remove from the heat and add a pinch of salt and black pepper.

4   Meanwhile, steam or blanch the broccoli in boiling water for 3–4 minutes until tender. Drain the broccoli and add to a non-stick frying pan over medium heat with the lime juice, soy sauce, maple syrup, and red pepper flakes. Cook for 2 minutes, stirring often, until the broccoli is glazed and sticky.

5   Serve the sticky broccoli over fluffy rice or noodles, topped with the crispy tofu, crushed peanuts, and lime zest.

Tips Make the broccoli sauce in advance or make more to freeze.

Swap broccoli for cauliflower or kale, carrots, sweet potatoes, sugar snap peas.

 2   10 mins   10 mins   Up to 3 days   Up to 1 month

Cauliflower Ragù

Cauliflower is one of my favorite ingredients to work with as it takes on flavors incredibly well and is so adaptable—it can be smooth and creamy or crunchy and crisp! It holds its texture perfectly in this rich and hearty ragù.

1 large cauliflower
2 Tbsp olive oil
2 Tbsp butter (see note on page 16)
1 onion, finely diced
3 garlic cloves, minced
1 Tbsp dried oregano
2–3 sprigs of fresh rosemary, leaves
  picked and finely chopped
⅔ cup tomato purée
7 Tbsp red wine
14 oz pappardelle
salt and black pepper

To serve
grated parmesan
a few fresh basil leaves

1 In a food processor, pulse the entire cauliflower in batches, including the core and leaves, until it resembles a rice texture. Tip into a bowl and set aside.

2 Heat the olive oil and butter in a large saucepan or Dutch oven over medium heat. Fry the onion with a generous pinch of salt and black pepper for 5 minutes, until soft. Add the garlic, dried oregano, and rosemary leaves, and cook for 1 minute. Add the tomato purée and cook, stirring well, for 2 minutes.

3 Add the riced cauliflower to the pan and stir until combined. Pour in the red wine and cook for 3–5 minutes, until the wine evaporates. Reduce the heat to low while you cook the pasta.

4 Cook the pappardelle in a large saucepan of salted boiling water according to the package instructions. When the pasta is cooked, use tongs to transfer the pasta from the water into the saucepan with the sauce, and toss together. Use a little of the pasta cooking liquid if you need to loosen the sauce. Swirl into bowls, top with parmesan and basil leaves, and serve.

 8
 5 mins
 20–25 mins
 Up to 5 days
 Up to 1 month

Spicy Baked Cauliflower Wings

These sticky and spicy cauliflower "wings" are a BIG fan favorite! Loaded with flavor, these are the best game-day snack or Friday night treat. Without the spicy hot sauce, they're crispy and crunchy on the outside and soft on the inside. With the sauce, they're a knockout!

1 large cauliflower, cut into 2-inch florets, core sliced, leaves separated

Batter
¼ cup chickpea or all-purpose flour
1 tsp ground turmeric
2 tsp chili powder
½ tsp black pepper
½ cup oat milk

Breadcrumb mix
⅔ cup breadcrumbs (homemade or panko)
2 tsp smoked paprika
½ tsp black pepper
generous pinch of salt

Quick buffalo sauce
2 Tbsp hot sauce
3 Tbsp tomato ketchup
2 Tbsp butter
2 Tbsp oat milk
1 Tbsp maple syrup
1 Tbsp cornstarch
2 tsp water

To serve
1 Tbsp toasted sesame seeds
1–2 spring onions, thinly sliced
1–2 Tbsp snipped fresh chives

1 Preheat the oven to 350°F. Line a baking pan with parchment paper.

2 In a bowl, combine all the batter ingredients and whisk until the mixture is smooth and slightly thick.

3 In a separate bowl, combine the breadcrumb mix.

4 Add the cauliflower pieces and leaves to the batter and mix to coat evenly. Next, place the cauliflower in the breadcrumb mix and coat evenly. Place the cauliflower in the lined baking pan and bake for 18–20 minutes, flipping halfway through, until the cauliflower is golden brown and crispy.

5 Meanwhile, make the buffalo sauce. In a pan over medium-low heat, stir together the hot sauce, ketchup, butter, oat milk, and maple syrup as it comes to a simmer, then cook for 2–3 minutes. In a small bowl, whisk together the cornstarch and water until well combined. Reduce the heat under the pan and stir in the cornstarch mixture for about 2 minutes, until smooth and silky. Remove from the heat and set aside.

6 Put the baked cauliflower in a large bowl, add a few spoonfuls of the buffalo sauce, and mix to coat evenly.

7 Serve hot, with a sprinkle of sesame seeds, spring onions, and chives.

 4–8 15 mins 20 mins Up to 1 month

Tips As a snack or side dish on their own, they're a 10/10—or serve with sticks of raw veg (carrots, celery) or in a sandwich roll or tortilla.

As a main dish for 4, serve with rice bowls, noodles, or tacos.

Swap cauliflower for broccoli.

Any leftovers are not fridge-friendly, as they will go soft and mushy.

The amount of batter and breadcrumbs will vary depending on the size of the cauliflower. If you need more batter, add a little more flour and milk.

Use chickpea flour for a gluten-free batter.

Air-fryer friendly.

Leafy Greens & Cruciferous

Sticky Cauliflower Wedges with Herby and Crunchy Rice

Sticky roasted cauliflower is the hero in this fun crowd-pleaser of a dish. It has an incredible combination of textures and flavors: wild rice adds bite, which goes with the fresh pop of pomegranate seeds and crunch of pistachios, which contrasts with the soft, caramelized cauliflower and fresh herbs. Every mouthful is an adventure! It's a dish to make when you want to show off.

2 cauliflowers (or 1 large)
1⅔ cups wild rice
⅔ cup roughly chopped fresh parsley
⅔ cup roughly chopped fresh mint
1 small pomegranate, seeds removed
zest of 1 lemon
2 Tbsp olive oil
2 tsp Dijon mustard
½ cup roasted pistachios, roughly chopped
2 Tbsp tahini
salt and black pepper
2 Tbsp sesame seeds, to serve

The glaze
2 Tbsp pomegranate molasses, plus more to drizzle (optional)
1 Tbsp maple syrup
2 Tbsp olive oil
2 tsp ground coriander
1 Tbsp harissa paste
juice of 1 lemon

1   Preheat the oven to 425°F.

2   In a small bowl, mix the ingredients for the glaze.

3   Cut the cauliflower into 4 large wedges through any remaining stem; you can leave the leaves on. Place the wedges on a baking sheet and use a brush to coat with the glaze. Season with salt and roast for 25 minutes, until charred and soft. Turn the cauliflower over and cook for a further 10 minutes.

4   Meanwhile, rinse the rice under cold running water until the water runs clear. Drain, then tip into a saucepan and cover with 2⅔ cups cold water. Bring to a boil, then turn down to a simmer, cover with a lid, and cook for 45 minutes, until tender. Remove from the heat and leave with the lid on to steam for 5 more minutes.

5   Stir in most of the herbs, the pomegranate seeds, zest of the lemon, the olive oil, and the mustard. Fold in most of the pistachios. Season well and set aside.

6   Put the tahini and a splash of water or lemon juice in a clean jar, seal the lid, and shake until smooth and drizzleable.

7   Spoon the cooked rice onto a large platter, topped with the charred cauliflower. Drizzle over the tahini, then scatter with the reserved herbs and pistachios and the sesame seeds. Drizzle with a little extra pomegranate molasses if you like!

Tip You can use broccoli or Romanesco instead of the cauliflower.

 4   20 mins   35 mins   1–3 days   Up to 1 month

Leafy Greens & Cruciferous

Roasted Cauliflower That's Anything But Boring

Cauliflower gets a bad rep for being bland but I see it more as a blank canvas! It's an incredibly versatile ingredient that can take on flavors well. Coating it in cornstarch before roasting produces a lovely crunchy coating, while the creamy mustard-maple-tahini sauce brings a sweet warmth. Seeds and chives add a pop of color and extra crunch, making this dish definitely not boring! A great main dish for two, either on its own or with tacos, pasta, or rice dishes, or perfect as a side dish for four.

1 large cauliflower, florets, leaves, and
  core separated
2 Tbsp olive oil
3 Tbsp cornstarch
generous pinch of salt
¼ tsp black pepper

Tahini mustard lemon sauce
1 Tbsp tahini
2 tsp Dijon mustard
juice of ½ lemon
1 tsp maple syrup

To serve
2 tsp toasted sesame seeds
snipped fresh chives

1   Preheat the oven to 400°F. Line a large baking sheet with parchment paper.

2   Put the cauliflower florets and leaves in a large bowl, slice the core and add that too, then add the olive oil and toss until evenly coated. Sprinkle with the cornstarch, salt, and black pepper and mix again.

3   Spread the cauliflower mixture on the lined baking sheet and roast for 17–20 minutes, until the cauliflower is just tender, a deep golden color, and beginning to brown at the edges.

4   Meanwhile, put all the sauce ingredients into a small jar or bowl, close the lid, and shake vigorously, or whisk until smooth.

5   Place the cauliflower back in the bowl. Drizzle over the tahini mustard lemon sauce and mix well.

6   Serve hot, on a large platter or individual plates or bowls. Sprinkle with toasted sesame seeds and chives.

Tips Don't crowd the baking sheet.

Use broccoli instead of cauliflower.

Make extra sauce for a rainy day: it will keep for up to 5 days in the fridge.

 2–4 | 10 mins | 20 mins | Up to 3 days | Up to 1 month | GF

Stems and Herbs Pesto

A high percentage of our food waste comes from the trimmings of veg and herbs, but there's so much flavor and goodness in those odds and ends. I've used broccoli stems here, but any green stalks—even those tough kale ribs—would work. Throw them all into this incredible, vibrant pesto and spread it in a sandwich (see page 93), toss into potato salads or any type of pasta, or use it instead of the tomato purée in my Best Roasted Potatoes on page 33.

1–2 broccoli stems, roughly chopped
4 garlic cloves, not peeled
7 oz malfada or fusilli pasta
2–3 large handfuls of mixed greens and soft herbs from the fridge, reserve some herbs for garnish
3 Tbsp toasted sunflower or pumpkin seeds, plus more to serve
3 Tbsp nutritional yeast
1 Tbsp grated parmesan, plus more to serve
zest and juice of 1 lemon
2 Tbsp extra-virgin olive oil, plus more for drizzling
1 Tbsp butter (see note on page 16)

1 Preheat the oven to 350°F. Line a baking sheet with parchment paper.

2 Put the broccoli stems and garlic on the baking sheet and roast for 10–12 minutes, until lightly charred and the broccoli stem is soft. Set aside to cool for 5 minutes before blending.

3 Meanwhile, bring a large pan of salted water to a boil, add the pasta, and cook until al dente. Drain, reserving 3 tablespoons of the pasta cooking water.

4 Into a food processor or blender, squeeze the garlic from its skin and blend with the broccoli stems, mixed greens and herbs, toasted seeds, nutritional yeast, parmesan, and lemon juice. With the motor running, stream in the extra-virgin olive oil and the reserved pasta water until the pesto is very smooth.

5 Return the drained pasta to its pan over low heat and gently stir in the butter. Add the pesto and lemon zest and stir to coat the pasta. Serve drizzled with olive oil and topped with more toasted seeds, parmesan, and mixed herbs.

Tips Leftover spinach, carrot tops, or celery leaves can all be included in place of herbs.

Store in a clean jar and pour in a thin layer of olive oil to preserve for up to 2 weeks.

Use gluten-free pasta if you prefer.

 2   10 mins   15 mins   3–4 days   Up to 1 month

Mighty Green Quiche

I know tofu can be a bit unpopular, but I love how incredibly versatile it is! Blended until smooth it perfectly replicates the rich, creamy egg mixture of a classic quiche. With spinach, kale, and feta folded in, you can cut a slice of this any time–for breakfast, lunch, or dinner–and leftovers taste even better the next day.

1 (8-inch) unbaked pie crust
1 Tbsp olive oil
4 cups roughly chopped spinach
3½ oz kale, leaves stripped from stems and roughly chopped
2 garlic cloves
1 tsp fennel seeds
1 tsp cumin seeds
10 oz extra-firm tofu
3–4 Tbsp oat milk
1 tsp cornstarch
1 oz feta, chunked (see note on page 16)
salt and black pepper

1   Chill the pie crust in the fridge for 20 minutes.

2   Preheat the oven to 350°F.

3   Meanwhile, heat the olive oil in a large frying pan over medium heat. Cook the spinach and kale for 4–5 minutes, until wilted and dark green. Crush the garlic into the pan and add the fennel seeds, cumin seeds, and a pinch of salt and black pepper. Stirring often, cook for 2 minutes, then remove from the heat.

4   Scrunch up a piece of parchment paper, un-scrunch it, then use it to line the pie crust. Fill with baking beans or rice, then pre-bake for 10–15 minutes. Remove the beans or rice, and cook for a further 5 minutes, until the pastry is pale and dry.

5   In a food processor or blender, process the tofu, oat milk, and cornstarch until smooth. Add the wilted greens mixture and blend again until well combined.

6   Tip the green mixture into the crust, then sprinkle the feta chunks on top. Bake for 30 minutes, until the filling is cooked through and the pastry is golden brown and cooked through. Set aside to cool for at least 15 minutes before serving.

Tip Can be made in advance; keep chilled. Want a slightly warmer quiche? Heat in the oven at 300°F for 5 minutes.

 4   50 mins–1 hour   Up to 5 days   Up to 1 month

Easy Spinach and Chickpea Curry

This curry is a weeknight must-make: quicker and much more satisfying than ordering and waiting for takeout. It's perfectly complemented with my easy Fragrant Flatbreads (page 206).

2 Tbsp vegetable oil
1 onion, chopped
4 garlic cloves, finely chopped
1 small piece fresh ginger, not peeled, grated
½ tsp brown mustard seeds
1 tsp cumin seeds or ground cumin
1 Tbsp madras curry powder
1 medium carrot, not peeled, roughly chopped
1 (14-oz) can chickpeas, drained and rinsed
1 cup cherry tomatoes, halved
½ tsp salt
¼ tsp black pepper
3 cups fresh spinach
1 (14-oz) can full-fat coconut milk

To serve
basmati rice
poppadoms
chopped fresh cilantro and mint
yogurt (see note on page 16)
Pickled Red Onion (page 267)
lime wedges

1 Heat the oil in a non-stick frying pan over medium heat and fry the onion for 5 minutes, until soft. Add the garlic, ginger, mustard seeds, cumin, and curry powder and cook for 2 minutes, stirring often, until fragrant.

2 Add the carrot, chickpeas, and tomatoes and cook for 8 minutes, until soft. Season with the salt and pepper.

3 Meanwhile, using a hand blender, blend the spinach and coconut milk until smooth.

4 Pour the green mixture into the frying pan, bring to a boil, and simmer over low heat for 10 minutes, stirring occasionally. Remove from the heat and leave to cool for a few minutes before serving.

5 Serve with fluffy basmati rice, poppadoms, fresh cilantro and mint, a dollop of yogurt, pickled red onion, and lime wedges.

 4
 10 mins
 25 mins
 Up to 3 days
 Up to 1 month
GF

Fridge Greens Fusilli

Go to your fridge and pull out those unused greens and get them involved in this warm, delicious, super-green pasta dish. You don't need to be meat-free to love how simple and delicious this is—that's why it's a fan favorite.

3 garlic cloves, not peeled
12 oz fusilli or pasta shells
10 oz mixed fresh greens (arugula, spinach, and/or kale, including the stems)
handful of fresh basil, including the stems
handful of fresh parsley, including the stems
2 Tbsp extra-virgin olive oil
1 cup grated parmesan, plus more to serve (see note on page 16)
2 Tbsp nutritional yeast
½ tsp salt
¼ tsp black pepper

1 Preheat the oven to 400°F. Put the garlic on a baking sheet and bake for 8 minutes until soft and lightly brown. Remove the skins; set aside.

2 Meanwhile, bring a large pan of salted water to a boil, add the pasta, and cook according to the package instructions. For the last 2 minutes of cooking the pasta, add the greens to a boiling water and cook until soft.

3 Using tongs, carefully lift out the veg and transfer to a blender. Add the roasted garlic, the herbs, olive oil, parmesan, nutritional yeast, salt, and black pepper. Blend until super-smooth and creamy.

4 Drain the pasta, reserving a few tablespoons of the cooking water.

5 Return the pasta to its pan along with the bright green sauce. If needed, loosen with a splash of the reserved cooking water, and stir to combine.

6 Serve the pasta in bowls, sprinkled with more grated parmesan.

Tip Use gluten-free pasta if you prefer.

 4   10 mins   15 mins   2–3 days   Up to 1 month

Leafy Greens & Cruciferous

Greens and Feta Tarte Soleil

Inspired by the flavors of a Greek spanakopita, this pastry centerpiece takes a little time to pull together but is so worth it. You can use any combination of leafy greens.

10 oz mixed leafy greens, roughly chopped (e.g., spinach, kale, arugula, lettuce, bok choy)
2 Tbsp chopped fresh dill
2 Tbsp chopped fresh mint
3 spring onions, thinly sliced
zest of 1 lemon
2½ oz feta, crumbled (see note on page 16)
¼ cup walnuts, roughly chopped
2 garlic cloves, grated
2 sheets puff pastry
all-purpose flour, for dusting
2 Tbsp olive oil
1 Tbsp oat milk
salt and black pepper

1   In a large bowl, combine the leafy greens, herbs, spring onions, lemon zest, feta, walnuts, garlic, a generous pinch of salt and ¼ teaspoon black pepper, and stir well to combine until it's a thick, spreadable paste. Set aside.

2   Place one of the pastry sheets on a lightly floured work surface (or still on its paper) and dust lightly with flour on both sides to keep it from sticking. If necessary, roll it out, but don't make it too thin. Place a plate, around 9 inches diameter, on top of the pastry and use a knife to cut around it. (Wrap and chill the leftover pastry to use in another recipe.) Lift the pastry circle onto a baking sheet, cover with a clean dry kitchen towel, and chill. Repeat with the second sheet of pastry and chill them both for about 10 minutes.

3   Spoon the filling onto one of the pastry circles, leaving a ⅜-inch border all the way around. Mix the olive oil and milk and brush around the edge of the pastry. Cover with the second pastry circle, and use your fingers to gently press and seal the two pieces of pastry together.

4   Now you're going to create the soleil part of your tart! Gently press a small glass (about 2-inch diameter) in the middle of the pastry. Using a large sharp knife, cut the pastry into quarters, but stop at the indent the glass made in the middle. Then cut each quarter into quarters, to make 16 "sun rays." Chill for 10–15 minutes.

5   Gently lift up one "sun ray" and twist it over 3 times. Bring the outer edge of the pastry roughly back to where it started. Repeat all around your sun. Chill again for 10–15 minutes.

6   Meanwhile, preheat the oven to 400°F.

7   Brush the pastry with the remaining olive oil and milk wash, sprinkle with salt and black pepper, and bake for about 35 minutes, until the pastry is a deep golden brown. Serve hot or at room temperature.

Tips If at any point the pastry becomes too soft, place it in the fridge for 10 minutes.

To reheat from frozen, bake at 300°F for 10–15 minutes until the pastry is crispy again.

 4
 30 mins
 35 mins
 1 day
 Up to 1 month

Leafy Greens & Cruciferous

Baking Sheet Pesto Pizza

A square of pizza is perfect for a snack, or serve two or three squares for a main meal for four. The tomato and cheese base is topped with a tasty kale pesto and handfuls of arugula and herbs. Depending on how far in advance you want to make this, you can choose how long to ferment the dough.

⅔ cup lukewarm water
1½ tsp active dry yeast, or 1 tsp instant yeast
1½ cups all-purpose flour, plus more for dusting
⅓ cup whole wheat or rye flour
generous pinch of salt
1 tsp sugar
2 Tbsp extra-virgin olive oil, plus more for drizzling
1 cup prepared tomato sauce (try my Simplest Tomato Sauce, page 87)
2½ oz parmesan cheese, grated, plus more to serve (see note on page 16)

Kale pesto
7 oz kale, leaves stripped from stems and roughly chopped
½ cup mixed nuts or seeds, toasted
3 Tbsp extra-virgin olive oil
2 Tbsp nutritional yeast
zest and juice of 1 lemon
½ tsp salt
¼ tsp black pepper

To serve
4 cups arugula
4 Tbsp chopped fresh herbs (e.g., basil, dill, parsley)
2 tsp balsamic vinegar
½ tsp red pepper flakes

Tips If using instant yeast, skip step 1. Just add to the flour in step 2, along with the warm water.

Check that you are not using yeast beyond its expiration date.

1 In a small bowl, whisk the warm water and yeast until the yeast has dissolved. Let it stand for 5 minutes. After this time the yeast should be foamy, which indicates that it is still active. (If you are using instant yeast, skip this step.)

2 Mix the flours, salt, sugar, and olive oil in a large bowl, then add the yeast and water. Using your hands, or a mixer fitted with a dough hook, knead until you have a sticky, shaggy dough. If it feels too wet, sprinkle in a bit more flour.

3 Spread a thin layer of olive oil (about 1 teaspoon) around the sides of the dough. Cover the bowl with a clean kitchen towel and leave to rise.

4 There are 3 ways to achieve the rise. Slow ferment in a large sealed container takes 24 hours in the fridge. Quick ferment takes 1½ hours in a warm place. Medium ferment takes 8 hours at room temperature.

5 Meanwhile, to make the kale pesto, put the kale in a bowl and cover with boiling water for 1–2 minutes, until soft and bright green. Drain, then cover the kale with cold water and leave for 2–3 minutes. Drain thoroughly, then place in a food processor or blender with the toasted nuts or seeds, olive oil, nutritional yeast, lemon juice and zest, salt, and pepper. Blend until slightly chunky; set aside.

6 Preheat the oven to its hottest setting (at least 475°F) for 20 minutes.

Fun facts Pizza is the first meal I can remember having (I think I was 4 years old). In my first job, I was the doughboy in a pizza restaurant. My DNA is 50 percent pizza.

 4–8   30 mins   15 mins   Up to 5 days   Up to 1 month

7   When the dough has risen, dust your hands with flour and tip the dough onto a floured surface. Starting at the center of the dough, using your fingertips, press out the dough to ¾-inch thickness, turning and gently stretching as you press. Put the dough onto a rimmed baking sheet, about 12 x 16 inches, and shape it to fit. Let it rest for 5–10 minutes.

8   With lightly oiled fingers, dimple the dough and then spread a thin layer (about 4 Tbsp) of the tomato sauce to the edges. Bake for 3 minutes.

9   Remove from the oven and add a slightly thicker layer of tomato sauce (remaining ¾ cup) and the parmesan. Lightly drizzle with extra-virgin olive oil, then bake for 8–10 minutes, or until the crust is golden brown and crispy.

10 Meanwhile, in a large bowl, toss the arugula and herbs with the balsamic vinegar and red pepper flakes.

11 Remove the pizza from the oven and leave to cool for 5 minutes. Lightly run a spatula around the edges of the crust, then transfer to a cutting board and cut into squares. Add more grated parmesan and spoonfuls of kale pesto and top with the arugula and herbs.

Crispy Kale Udon Noodles and Peanut Butter Miso Dressing

Everyone needs a quick, hearty noodle dish in their lives, and this is it! Using mostly ingredients already in your cupboard, it's a perfect balance of fresh, crunch, heat, and creaminess—and it is 100 percent satisfying. Kale provides a crispy layer, but if you don't have kale, use steamed spinach or peas instead and skip the baking step.

5 cups kale, leaves stripped from stems and roughly torn
2 Tbsp extra-virgin olive oil
2 Tbsp nutritional yeast
½ tsp salt
7 oz udon noodles
1 Tbsp smooth peanut butter
1 Tbsp grated fresh ginger
1 garlic clove, grated
1 tsp toasted sesame oil
1 Tbsp white miso
zest and juice of 1 lime
½ tsp red pepper flakes
1 tsp maple syrup or light brown sugar
¼ cup toasted peanuts or almonds, crushed
1 baby cucumber, cut into thin matchsticks
½ tsp sesame seeds, toasted
pinch of salt

Tips Use the kale stems for Fridge Greens Fusilli (page 160) or Stems and Herbs Pesto (page 156).

More bulk? Add crispy tofu from page 105.

Make ahead: prepare the sauce the day before or double the quantity to use again later in the week.

Look for gluten-free noodles if you prefer.

1 Preheat the oven to 300°F. Line 2 baking sheets with parchment paper.

2 In a large bowl, toss and lightly massage the kale with the olive oil, nutritional yeast, and salt until evenly coated.

3 Spread the kale over the baking sheets and cook for about 8 minutes, flipping halfway through, until the kale is crispy and dark around the edges.

4 Meanwhile, bring a large pan of salted water to a boil and cook the noodles according to the package instructions. Drain thoroughly. Transfer the noodles to a large bowl.

5 In a separate bowl, whisk together the peanut butter, ginger, garlic, sesame oil, miso, lime juice and half the zest, the red pepper flakes, and maple syrup, until smooth. If the dressing is too thick, add 1 teaspoon of water to loosen. Pour most of the dressing over the noodles and mix gently to coat.

6 Fold in half of the crispy kale, then serve topped with the remaining crispy kale, the crushed nuts, cucumber, remaining lime zest, the rest of the peanut butter miso dressing, and the sesame seeds and salt.

 2   15 mins   10 mins   1–3 days   Up to 1 month

Super Green Pancakes

A green smoothie magically turns into a stack of pancakes—that's my kind of breakfast! Colorful, healthy, and fun. If you're not wild about the taste of spinach, don't fret—you won't taste it. A fan favorite and soon to be yours. Have fun with the toppings!

3 cups fresh spinach
2 ripe bananas
1⅓ cups oat milk
1¼ cups all-purpose flour
1½ tsp baking powder
½ tsp ground cinnamon
½ tsp salt
1 tsp vanilla extract
2–3 tsp vegetable oil (optional)

To serve
your choice of toppings: fresh fruits, yogurt, nut butter, toasted coconut flakes, toasted pumpkin seeds, maple syrup

1 In a food processor or blender, blend the spinach, bananas, and milk until smooth.

2 In a large bowl, add the flour, baking powder, cinnamon, and salt and stir to combine. Add the spinach and banana mixture, along with the vanilla, and stir until the batter is thick but pourable. If too thick, add a small splash of milk to loosen the batter. If too loose, stir in 1 tablespoon of flour at a time to thicken slightly.

3 Heat a non-stick frying pan over medium heat (depending on your pan, you may like to add a little oil to prevent the pancakes from sticking). Once the pan is hot, add half-ladlefuls of the batter to make small pancakes. Cook for 1–1½ minutes, until the pancakes rise and bubbles appear on the surface. Flip and cook on the other side for 1–2 minutes. Keep warm while you cook the remaining batter.

4 To serve, stack the pancakes and add your favorite toppings. I went for fresh blueberries, coconut yogurt, almond butter, toasted coconut flakes, pumpkin seeds, and a drizzle of maple syrup.

Tips Do not flatten the pancakes with the spatula as they cook: allow them to rise to nice, fluffy pancakes.

Save leftover batter to make savory crepes for dinner.

Use gluten-free flour and baking powder if you need a gluten-free option.

12 pancakes   5 mins   10–15 mins   Up to 3 days   Up to 1 month

6– Fungi & Alliums

Mushrooms
Onion
Garlic

Mushroom Ravioli with Tofu Asparagus Purée

Don't be put off making this because you think homemade pasta is too difficult. Just follow the steps and you'll be surprised how easy it is—it's failproof! The ravioli has a rich mushroom filling and it's served on an elegant asparagus cream, finished with a parsley-lemon oil. Make it for friends and family when you want to really impress.

Pasta
3¼ cups 00 flour, plus more for dusting (or semolina for dusting)
pinch of ground turmeric
1 cup aquafaba
oat milk (optional)
salt

Filling
2 Tbsp olive oil
14 oz mixed mushrooms, roughly chopped
2 garlic cloves, grated
1 Tbsp thyme leaves
7 oz cream cheese, softened (see note on page 16)
zest of 1 lemon

Asparagus cream
12 oz asparagus
12 oz silken tofu
½ cup fresh parsley, stems chopped, leaves finely chopped
zest and juice of 1 lemon
2 Tbsp nutritional yeast
2 Tbsp tahini
2 tsp Dijon mustard
4 Tbsp olive oil
2 garlic cloves, finely sliced
4 Tbsp toasted pine nuts, to serve

1   First make the pasta. Add the flour to a bowl or a stand mixer, along with the turmeric and a pinch of salt, and mix well. Make a well in the middle of the flour and pour in the aquafaba. Use a fork to draw it together. Don't worry if it looks a little dry, it'll come together. Use your hands to knead the mixture, then tip it out onto a lightly floured work surface and knead for a further minute until you have a soft ball of dough. Place in a bowl, cover with a damp clean kitchen towel, and set aside.

2   Make the mushroom filling. Heat the oil in a frying pan over high heat. Add the mushrooms and a generous pinch of salt, and fry for 5–10 minutes, until the mushrooms are golden and all their liquid has evaporated from the pan. Add the garlic and thyme leaves, cook for 1 minute, then remove from the heat and combine in a bowl with the cream cheese and lemon zest, stirring to combine. Set aside to cool or pop it in the fridge until you're ready to fill your pasta.

3   Make the asparagus cream. Bring a pan of salted water to a boil. Remove any very woody ends from the asparagus (save them for stock or blend them to make a soup). Cut the asparagus stems in half, separating the stems from the tips; set the tips aside for later. Cook the stems in the boiling water for 3–5 minutes, until a knife slides through them easily. Drain and add to a high-speed blender along with the tofu, parsley stems, the lemon juice, nutritional yeast, tahini, and Dijon mustard. Blend until smooth, set aside, and keep warm.

 4

 40 mins

 15–25 mins

 Up to 5 days

 Up to 1 month

4 Line a tray with a little flour or semolina and lightly flour the work surface. Cut the pasta dough into quarters. Take one quarter and roll through your pasta-making machine—you want to take it to 1⁄16-inch thickness, so it's thick enough to hold the filling. Roll to a sheet approx. 16 inches long, then cut the sheet into 3 rectangles on the work surface.

5 For each rectangle, add 2–3 heaped tablespoons of the filling on one side, leaving a generous border, then fold the other side over and press to seal with your fingers. Use a knife or ravioli cutter to cut the edges, and use a little oat milk to help them stick if you think it needs it. Set aside on the lined tray and repeat with the other rectangles, making 3 large ravioli per person. Repeat with the rest of the dough.

6 Bring a large pan of salted water to a boil. Meanwhile, add the 4 tablespoons of olive oil to a large frying pan over a high heat. Add the reserved asparagus tips and fry for 2 minutes, then add the garlic, fry for 1 minute, then remove from the heat. Add the parsley leaves to the pan along with the lemon zest. Season well.

7 Drop the pasta into a boiling water and cook for 3–4 minutes, until soft, then use a slotted spoon to slosh them into the asparagus pan.

8 Spread the asparagus cream in the bottom of your serving bowls. Top with the pasta and spoon over the asparagus tips and parsley-lemon oil from the pan. Scatter with the toasted pine nuts and serve.

Tips When you seal the pasta, make sure to press around the filling to release any air otherwise it could burst open as it cooks.

You can, of course, use bought pasta and serve it with the mushroom and asparagus cream sauce.

Fun fact The first time I made pasta I was 5 years old, then I didn't make it for 20 years.

Crispy Mushroom Risotto

This risotto is rich, creamy, and packed with flavor, with a topping of crispy mushrooms. Don't worry if you can't find shiitake mushrooms: I've made this risotto with chestnut mushrooms and it was still delicious.

1 Tbsp + 1 tsp olive oil
3 Tbsp butter (see note on page 16)
1 onion, finely chopped
2 celery stalks, finely chopped
3 garlic cloves, thinly sliced
10 oz shiitake mushrooms, cut into
  ¼-inch slices
1 tsp brown sugar
2 tsp soy sauce or tamari
2 tsp chopped fresh thyme
1 cup arborio rice
¾ cup +1 Tbsp dry white wine
3½ cups veg stock, warmed
2 cups grated parmesan
zest and juice of 1 lemon
2 Tbsp chopped fresh parsley
salt and black pepper

1   Preheat the oven to 400°F. Line a baking sheet with parchment paper.

2   In a large pan, heat 1 tablespoon of olive oil and 2 tablespoons of butter over low heat; add the onion, celery, and garlic; season with salt and black pepper; and cook for about 10 minutes, stirring occasionally, until soft.

3   Meanwhile, put the mushrooms in a large bowl, add 1 teaspoon of olive oil, the brown sugar, soy sauce, and 1 teaspoon of chopped thyme and toss to combine. Spread the mushrooms evenly over the lined baking sheet and bake for 15–20 minutes, flipping halfway through, until crispy and slightly charred. Remove from the oven and set aside.

4   Increase the heat under the onion mixture to medium, add the rice and stir to coat, then add the wine and cook for 2–3 minutes, stirring occasionally.

5   Once the wine has almost evaporated, add a ladleful of stock to the rice mixture and stir until absorbed. Continue to add the stock, a ladleful at a time, stirring continuously, for about 30 minutes, until the rice is cooked. You may need to adjust the heat to keep the mixture at a steady simmer.

6   Remove the risotto from the heat and stir in half of the parmesan, the lemon juice, half of the crispy mushrooms, 1 tablespoon of butter, 1 tablespoon of the chopped parsley, and the remaining thyme.

7   Serve in bowls, topped with the remaining crispy mushrooms, parsley, parmesan, lemon zest, and a pinch of salt and black pepper.

Tip Use tamari (rather than soy sauce) for a gluten-free dish.

 4   15 mins   45 mins   1 day   Up to 1 month

Pulled Mushroom Tacos with Avocado and Tomato Salsa

The hero of this dish is of course the king oyster mushrooms, which when shredded almost exactly resemble the texture of succulent pulled pork. I once worked in a Spanish-Asian restaurant in New York that served incredible pulled pork tacos, and I wanted to replicate the meatiness and flavor of that special dish. Top the tacos with a generous amount of cooling creamy avocado salsa.

10 oz king oyster mushrooms
4 Tbsp vegetable oil
2 garlic cloves, finely chopped
1 Tbsp ancho chile paste
½ tsp ground cumin
½ tsp chili powder
generous pinch of salt and black
  pepper
8–12 corn or flour tortillas, warmed,
  to serve

Avocado salsa
1 large tomato, diced
2 spring onions, thinly sliced
1 jalapeño pepper, seeded and finely
  chopped
1 large avocado, diced
4 Tbsp chopped fresh cilantro,
  including stems
zest and juice of 1 lime
pinch of salt

1   First, make the avocado salsa by gently folding all the ingredients together in a small bowl. Leave to one side while you prepare the pulled mushrooms.

2   Shred the oyster mushrooms. Heat the oil in a large non-stick frying pan over medium-high heat and cook half of the mushrooms in a single layer for 10–12 minutes, stirring occasionally, until the edges start to char. For the last 3–5 minutes, add half the garlic and ancho chile paste, stirring to combine. Using tongs, transfer the mushrooms to a bowl. Repeat with the rest of the mushrooms.

3   Once the second batch of mushrooms is cooked, toss all the mushrooms with the cumin, chili powder, salt, and black pepper.

4   Fill the warm tortillas with the mushroom mixture and top with the avocado salsa.

Tipc Use gluten-free corn tortillas if you prefer.

You can add any other leftover mushrooms to the mix.

 2–4   10 mins   20–25 mins   Up to 3 days

Easy Bean and Mushroom Casserole

Make this bean and mushroom casserole as a side dish, or make ahead to enjoy as a main for those evenings when you don't have time to cook. Comforting and delicious, topped with golden cheese and crispy breadcrumbs, this is one of my favorite dishes to make.

14 oz chestnut or porcini mushrooms, cut into ⅜-inch slices
4 garlic cloves, finely chopped
2 Tbsp extra-virgin olive oil
1 tsp dried oregano
1 (14-oz) can cannellini beans, rinsed and drained
1 (14-oz) can chopped tomatoes
2 tsp roughly chopped fresh thyme
½ cup shredded mozzarella (see note on page 16)
1½ cups breadcrumbs (homemade from a stale loaf)
salt and black pepper
garlic bread (try my Cheesy Garlic Bread, page 199), to serve

1   Preheat the oven to 375°F.

2   In an ovenproof frying pan, combine the mushrooms with half of the garlic, the olive oil, oregano, and a generous pinch of salt and black pepper. Cook over medium heat for about 10 minutes, stirring often, until the mushrooms are lightly golden brown and they begin to reduce in size.

3   Remove the pan from the heat. Stir in the beans, tomatoes, thyme, and the remaining garlic. Scatter over the mozzarella. Sprinkle the breadcrumbs over the top and transfer to the oven to bake for 20–25 minutes, until the mixture is bubbling and the cheese is lightly golden brown.

4   Leave to cool for a few minutes before serving with my cheesy garlic bread.

Tip Use gluten-free breadcrumbs if you need a gluten-free option, or use my Crispy Garlic Breadcrumbs from page 30 or the garlicky breadcrumbs on page 90.

 4–6   10 mins   35 mins   Up to 3 days   Up to 1 month

Mushroom Masala and Crispy Cardamom Rice

I don't want to say that this dish was created because of my love of alliteration . . . but it may have played a part! Chunky mushrooms and juicy tomatoes are all wrapped up in the familiar aromatics of a rich masala sauce. Served with baked coconut rice, spiked with cloves, cardamom, and cinnamon, this has quickly become a weeknight go-to.

2 Tbsp neutral oil (e.g., peanut, sunflower, or vegetable)
1 onion, finely diced
3 garlic cloves, minced
1 Tbsp grated fresh ginger
1 tsp ground turmeric
1 tsp ground cumin
1 Tbsp garam masala
1 tsp chili powder
1 (14-oz) can chopped tomatoes
14 oz mixed mushrooms (I use an exotic mix; any larger ones sliced)
½ cup full-fat coconut cream
1 lime, cut in half

Baked rice
1½ cups basmati or jasmine rice
1⅔ cups coconut milk
1 cup veg stock
4–6 cardamom pods
1 stick cinnamon or 1 tsp ground cinnamon
salt and black pepper

To serve
4 Tbsp chopped fresh mint
4 Tbsp chopped fresh cilantro
coconut cream or yogurt
Fragrant Flatbreads (page 206)

1 Preheat the oven to 350°F.

2 Rinse the rice under cold running water until the water runs clear. Drain, then tip into a baking dish with the coconut milk, stock, cardamom, and cinnamon. Season with salt and black pepper, cover with foil, and bake for 40–45 minutes, until the rice is cooked through and all the liquid has been absorbed. Remove from the oven and set aside.

3 Meanwhile, heat 1 tablespoon of the oil in a large saucepan over medium heat. Fry the onion with a generous pinch of salt for 5 minutes, until soft. Add the garlic, ginger, and the spices, and cook for 2 minutes, stirring occasionally. Add the chopped tomatoes, reduce to a simmer, cover with a lid, and cook for 20 minutes.

4 In a frying pan over high heat, dry-fry the mushrooms, stirring often, for 5–7 minutes, until the mushrooms have released their liquid. Reduce the heat to medium, add the remaining oil, and cook, stirring, for 3–5 minutes until slightly crispy around the edges.

5 Stir the coconut cream into the curry, followed by the crispy mushrooms. Taste and season well, adding the juice of half the lime. Cut the remaining lime half into wedges to serve.

6 Serve the curry with the rice, scattered with the fresh herbs and drizzled with coconut cream. Serve with flatbreads and lime wedges on the side.

 4 10 mins 40–45 mins Up to 5 days Up to 1 month **GF**

Fungi & Alliums

Mushroom Pad Thai

I love pad Thai! I think it's because of the unbeatable combination of crunchy bean sprouts and peanuts, silky noodles, and fresh herbs with the salty sweet-and-tangy sauce and fiery ginger. In my version, I've used two types of mushrooms for extra texture and flavor. Pulled together quickly, it's like magic happening in the kitchen.

7 oz flat rice noodles
1 Tbsp vegetable oil
10 oz mushrooms, quartered
3 spring onions, finely sliced
2 garlic cloves, finely sliced
1 Tbsp fresh ginger, cut into
   matchsticks
5¼ oz bean sprouts
salt and black pepper

Sauce
zest and juice of 1–2 limes
2 Tbsp tamarind paste
4 Tbsp soy sauce or tamari
2 Tbsp brown sugar
1 Tbsp white miso

To serve
a handful of salted peanuts, crushed
4 Tbsp fresh cilantro leaves
4 Tbsp fresh mint leaves

1 Cover the rice noodles with boiling water and set aside for 10–15 minutes, until softened. Drain the noodles, rinse, and leave to sit in a bowl of cold water (this stops them clumping together).

2 Make the sauce. Whisk all the ingredients together; add the zest and juice of 1 lime to begin with, then taste and add the zest and juice of the other if needed.

3 Heat the oil in a large frying pan or wok over high heat. Add the mushrooms with a generous pinch of salt and fry for 5–10 minutes, until golden.

4 Add most of the spring onions, the garlic, and the ginger and toss well. Use tongs to add the rice noodles, along with the sprouts. Keep tossing, then add the sauce and coat well. Taste and season with salt and black pepper.

5 Serve topped with the crushed peanuts, fresh herb leaves, and remaining spring onions. Serve with any leftover lime, cut into wedges, on the side.

Tip Use tamari (rather than soy sauce) for a gluten-free dish.

 4 20 mins 15 mins Up to 5 days Up to 1 month **GF**

Takeout-Style Mushrooms and "Egg" Noodles

Mushrooms are the hero of this satisfying sweet-and-salty dish, so if you're craving "egg" noodles, it's so much better than ordering in. The secret is the baking soda, which magically combines with the starchy water to produce that distinctive egg-like flavor. To make the meal more substantial, top with crispy tofu or add more veg.

5¼ oz shiitake mushrooms
1 tsp olive oil
2 tsp soy sauce or tamari
2 garlic cloves, finely chopped
1 tsp maple syrup
7 oz spaghetti
2 tsp baking soda

Sauce
3 Tbsp soy sauce or tamari
2 Tbsp toasted sesame oil
1 Tbsp smooth peanut butter
2 tsp rice vinegar
2 tsp sugar
1 Tbsp grated fresh ginger
1 tsp red pepper flakes

To serve
⅓ cup roasted peanuts, chopped
1 baby cucumber, cut into matchsticks

1 Preheat the oven to 400°F. Line a baking sheet with parchment paper.

2 Put the mushrooms in a bowl, add the olive oil, soy sauce, garlic, and maple syrup and toss to combine. Spread evenly on the baking sheet and bake for about 12 minutes, until crispy. Remove from the heat and set aside.

3 Meanwhile, bring a pan of water to a boil and cook the spaghetti for about 10 minutes or until tender and cooked all the way through. About halfway through cooking, add 1 teaspoon of baking soda at a time—it will make the water bubble. Turn off the heat and let the spaghetti sit in the water for 5–7 minutes, until doubled in thickness. Drain and place in a bowl.

4 Put all the sauce ingredients into a small jar or bowl; close the lid and shake vigorously, or whisk until smooth. Pour half of the sauce over the noodles and toss.

5 Serve the noodles in bowls, topped with the crispy mushrooms, chopped peanuts, cucumber, and a drizzle of the sauce.

Tips Use gluten-free pasta and tamari (rather than soy sauce) for a gluten-free dish.

You can use any type of pasta or noodle for this.

Be mindful when you add the baking soda; it will bubble up like a science project—you may need to reduce the heat to prevent spillage.

 2   10 mins   20 mins   Up to 3 days   Up to 1 month

Meaty Mushroom Burgers

These burgers are for the bros in your life! Already chunky and meaty from the ground "meat," I've made them next-level juicy and satisfying with extra mushrooms. Perfect for barbecues, picnics, and relaxed summertime vibes, pile these high with toppings and make them your own. Beer keg optional.

1 Tbsp flaxseed or chia seeds
7 oz chestnut or portobello
  mushrooms, roughly chopped
2 Tbsp olive oil
1 onion, finely diced
2 garlic cloves, grated
10 oz plant-based ground "meat"
2 Tbsp nutritional yeast
⅓ cup breadcrumbs
4 slices smoked Gouda (see note on
  page 16)
salt and black pepper

To serve
4 Tbsp mayonnaise
4 burger buns
2 Little Gem lettuce, leaves pulled
  apart
4 tomatoes, sliced
pickles or gherkins
1 red onion, sliced
ketchup
mustard

1 In a small bowl, combine the flaxseed with 1 tablespoon of water. Set aside to thicken to a jelly-like consistency.

2 In a large frying pan over high heat, dry-fry the mushrooms for 5–7 minutes, until the mushrooms have released most of their liquid. This gives them a slightly meatier texture. Place in a bowl.

3 In the same frying pan, reduce the heat to medium, add 1 tablespoon of oil, and fry the onion with a generous pinch each of salt and pepper for 5 minutes, until soft. Add the garlic, cook for a further minute, then tip into the bowl with the mushrooms. Add the ground "meat," flaxseed mixture, nutritional yeast, and breadcrumbs.

4 Use your hands to bring the mixture together, then shape into 4 large burger patties. Flatten them a little in the palms of your hands, then place on a baking sheet lined with parchment paper and chill in the fridge for 30 minutes to firm up.

5 When ready to serve, heat the remaining oil in a large frying pan over a medium-high heat. Fry the burgers for 3–4 minutes on one side, then flip over and immediately top with a slice of the cheese. Cook for 3–4 minutes, until the cheese is melting. Encourage the cheese to melt by adding a splash of water to the pan and covering with a lid!

6 Spread the mayo on the base of the burger buns, top with the burger patties, followed by lettuce, tomato, pickles, and red onion. Spread some ketchup and mustard on the top bun and close.

Tip You could make 8 smaller patties instead and serve up mini meaty sliders!

 4   15 mins   20 mins Up to 5 days   Up to 1 month

Extra Crunchy Onion Rings

A fan favorite, with over 2 million views, these are the best crispy onion rings you'll ever make. Don't be tempted to take them out of the oven too soon: bake until they're golden brown and crispy. These onion rings never get the chance to sit around for long.

2–3 large onions
flaky sea salt for sprinkling

Batter
½ cup flour or gluten-free flour
⅔ cup milk of your choice
1 Tbsp apple cider vinegar
1 tsp baking powder
½ tsp chili powder
¼ tsp ground turmeric
black pepper

Breadcrumb mix
1⅔ cups panko breadcrumbs
2 Tbsp cornmeal
½ tsp chili powder
¼ tsp thyme (fresh or dried)
¼ tsp ground turmeric
black pepper

1 Preheat the oven to 425°F. Line a baking sheet with parchment paper.

2 Slice the ends off each onion and carefully slice the onions into ⅜-inch rounds. Separate the rounds into individual rings.

3 To make the batter, in a mixing bowl, whisk all the ingredients together with a pinch of black pepper until smooth and pourable.

4 For the breadcrumb mix, mix all the dry ingredients with a pinch of black pepper, then divide between 2 bowls: keep one bowl to the side—this will come in handy when the first bowl of breadcrumbs gets a bit soggy from the batter.

5 Dip each onion ring in the batter and allow any excess batter to drip off. Then place the onion ring in the breadcrumb mix and coat well. Place the coated onion rings on the lined baking sheet and bake for 8–10 minutes, or until golden brown and crispy.

6 Serve immediately with a sprinkle of flaky sea salt and a dipping sauce of your choice. I eat mine with ketchup or mayo.

Tips Perfect alongside a salad.

Can be made in an air-fryer.

Save the onion skins and trimmed ends in a bag or container in the fridge or freezer to make a stock (page 260).

Don't store any leftovers in the fridge—they will go soft.

 4   10 mins   10 mins

Caramelized Onion and Miso Mushroom Rigatoni

I'm a big fan of pasta and in this dish, I wanted to bring it together with all the flavors of a classic French onion soup! Sweet, caramelized onions, thyme, and a little mustard and red pepper flakes for heat, with added mushrooms for a chunkier, meatier texture. It's topped with crispy, fried breadcrumbs and parmesan—just like the melted cheese toasts you get on the traditional soup.

2 Tbsp olive oil
3 Tbsp butter (see note on page 16)
3 onions, thinly sliced
1 shallot, thinly sliced
2 Tbsp chopped fresh thyme, plus more to serve
½ tsp salt
¼ tsp black pepper
1 tsp sugar (optional)
pinch of red pepper flakes
2 tsp white wine vinegar
8 oz white button or chestnut mushrooms, sliced
2 garlic cloves, finely chopped
12 oz rigatoni or pasta of your choice
1¼ cups breadcrumbs (homemade or panko)
1 tsp Dijon mustard
1 Tbsp white miso (optional)
2 Tbsp roughly chopped fresh parsley
2 Tbsp grated parmesan

1 Heat 1 tablespoon of the olive oil and the butter in a large non-stick frying pan over medium heat until the butter has melted. Stir in the onions and shallot, then leave to cook undisturbed for 3 minutes. If the onions and shallot start to brown, lower the heat.

2 Stir in the thyme, salt, pepper, sugar, if using, and red pepper flakes. Continue cooking over a low heat for 15–20 minutes, stirring every 3 minutes, until the onions have collapsed and resemble onion jam.

3 Add the vinegar and mushrooms and cook for 3–5 minutes, until the mushrooms are soft. Stir in the garlic for the last minute of cooking.

4 Meanwhile, bring a large pan of salted water to a boil and cook the pasta according to the package instructions. Drain, reserving 2 tablespoons of the pasta cooking water. Place the pasta in a large bowl.

5 Heat the remaining olive oil in a small pan over medium heat. Cook the breadcrumbs for about 3 minutes, stirring often, until golden brown and crispy.

6 Add the mustard, miso, if using, and reserved pasta water to the onion and mushroom mixture, stir well to combine, then fold into the pasta.

7 Serve in bowls, with a sprinkling of crispy breadcrumbs, fresh thyme, parsley, and grated parmesan.

Tips Use gluten-free pasta and breadcrumbs if you prefer.

If you have some of my Garlic and Lemon Pangrattato (page 200) to hand, use that instead of frying the breadcrumbs in step 5.

 4
 15 mins
 30–35 mins
 Up to 3 days
 Up to 1 month

Quick Garlic Chile Ramen

I asked my audience how much time they usually have to cook, and most people came back saying 15 minutes! So here we are: a recipe that I think is actually on the table in closer to 10 minutes. Sautéing the spring onions brings out their sweetness, while the fresh ginger keeps things fiery. This is such a simple dish for when you're short on time but don't want to compromise on taste. Add crispy tofu, such as my Killer Tofu "Ground Beef" on page 128, or steamed spinach, broccoli, or peas if you want to bulk it up.

1 small piece fresh ginger, cut into thin matchsticks
4 garlic cloves, finely grated
6 spring onions, very thinly sliced
½ cup vegetable oil
2 Tbsp soy sauce, tamari or teriyaki sauce
1 Tbsp rice vinegar
1 tsp toasted sesame oil
½ tsp sugar
½ tsp black pepper
7 oz ramen noodles
1–2 tsp toasted white or black sesame seeds
Quick Garlic Chile Oil (page 265), or crushed chiles in vinegar (store-bought)
lime wedges, to serve

1 Put the ginger, garlic, and half of the spring onions in a large bowl.

2 Heat the oil in a frying pan over medium-high heat for 2 minutes. Pour the hot oil over the spring onion mixture and set aside for 1–2 minutes, until the spring onions are vibrantly green and soft. Stir in the soy sauce, vinegar, sesame oil, sugar, and black pepper. Set aside for 10 minutes.

3 Meanwhile, cook the noodles according to the package instructions. Drain well, then toss the noodles in a few spoonfuls of the spring onion sauce.

4 Serve with lime wedges and topped with toasted sesame seeds, the remaining spring onions, and some quick garlic chile oil or crushed chiles in vinegar.

 2–4   10 mins   10 mins   Up to 3 days   Up to 1 month

Fungi & Alliums

Broccolini and Cream Cheese on Toast with Pickled Stems

Slightly softened, charred Broccolini sits on a cool, cream cheese base, then is topped with the sweet-acidic crunch of the Broccolini stem pickle. Two different preps of Broccolini for the price of one! Serve one toast each as a starter or cut into smaller pieces as a party appetizer.

14 oz Broccolini
juice of 2 lemons
2 Tbsp drained capers
1 shallot, finely diced
1 tsp sugar
2 Tbsp olive oil, plus more to serve
4 thick slices of sourdough bread
4 oz cream cheese (see note on page 16)
3 Tbsp pine nuts, toasted and roughly chopped
handful of fresh dill or parsley, finely chopped
pinch of red pepper flakes
salt and black pepper

1   Finely slice the stems of the Broccolini, leaving 4 inches at the top. Put the stems in a bowl with the lemon juice, capers, shallot, sugar, and a pinch of salt. Toss everything together and set aside.

2   Preheat the broiler to high. Put the Broccolini heads onto a baking sheet. Drizzle with 1 tablespoon of the olive oil and season with salt and black pepper. Broil for about 8 minutes, depending on thickness, until slightly charred.

3   Meanwhile, toast the slices of bread. Spread each slice of toast with 2 tablespoons of the cream cheese, top with the charred Broccolini, and spoon the pickled stems over the top. Finish with the toasted pine nuts, herbs, a pinch of red pepper flakes, and a drizzle of olive oil.

 4   10 mins   10 mins   Up to 3 days

Cheesy Garlic Bread

With the perfect butter, cheese, garlic ratio, and deliciously soft bread in the middle, make this recipe once and I guarantee you'll keep coming back to it! Dunk this cheesy garlic bread in soups or stews, or serve alongside pasta or salad.

6 garlic cloves, grated
6½ Tbsp butter, at room temperature
  (see note on page 16)
1 tsp Dijon mustard
2½ oz parmesan, grated
zest and juice of ½ lemon
2 tsp dried or chopped fresh oregano
2 tsp chopped fresh parsley
½ tsp red pepper flakes
½ tsp salt
½ tsp black pepper
1 large baguette or any loaf-style bread

1 In a small bowl, mash the garlic, butter, mustard, parmesan, lemon juice and zest, oregano, parsley, and red pepper flakes. Season with the salt and pepper.

2 Preheat the broiler to medium. Line a baking sheet with parchment paper.

3 Slice the baguette in half lengthwise, then into quarters. Place cut side down on the lined baking sheet and broil for 2 minutes. Leave to cool on the baking tray for 2 minutes, then spread the cut sides with the garlic butter. Broil for about 3 minutes, until beginning to bubble. Leave to cool slightly before slicing into 2-inch pieces and serving.

Tips Save any leftover garlic butter and toss with pasta, serve on steamed veg, or use to sauté mushrooms to go on toast.

To reheat leftover garlic bread (you won't see this in my home!), place on a baking sheet in a preheated oven and broil for 5–7 minutes until warm and crunchy.

 8   10 mins   5 mins   Up to 5 days   Up to 1 month

Garlic and Lemon Pangrattato

Italians often top their dishes with dried breadcrumbs to add a layer of crunch, and it's a great use for any type of stale leftover bread. I use my garlicky version—made with cornflakes for even more crunchy flavor!—scattered over pasta or noodle dishes, in salads, and on gratins. To give it an Asian-style spin add a little freshly grated ginger with the garlic and substitute lime for the lemon.

3 Tbsp butter (see note on page 16)
4–5 garlic cloves, grated
½ tsp dried thyme
1⅓ cups breadcrumbs (homemade or panko)
1 cup unsweetened cornflakes, crushed (optional)
zest of 1 lemon
1 Tbsp finely chopped fresh parsley
salt and black pepper

1   Melt the butter in a non-stick frying pan over medium-low heat. Stir in the garlic and cook for 2 minutes.

2   Add the dried thyme, breadcrumbs, and cornflakes, if using, and stir to coat in the garlicky butter. Keeping a careful eye on it so it doesn't burn and, stirring often, cook the breadcrumb mixture for 4–5 minutes, until golden brown. Remove from heat and toss with lemon zest and fresh parsley.

3   Season with salt and black pepper and spread on a large platter to cool. Store in an airtight container for up to 7 days.

4   Serve the pangrattato over any pasta dish or over simply cooked veg dishes.

Tips Use gluten-free breadcrumbs and cornflakes if you prefer.

Save the crumbs from the bottom of your cornflake box to add to this recipe.

 4–6   5 mins   10 mins   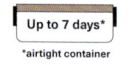 Up to 7 days*
*airtight container

Fungi & Alliums

Rich Garlic and Onion Broth

Onions and garlic are often "forgotten," and when you find them, they have often softened or have green shoots emerging. You can remove the green shoots and carry on, but I take this as an opportunity to make a supremely savory stock. The flavor is intense and delicious. Great to keep on hand and stored in the fridge or freezer. Use in recipes that ask for stock, such as my Crispy Mushroom Risotto (page 178) or Creamy Leek and Parsnip Soup (page 22), or add noodles for a warming and comforting meal.

1 garlic head, not peeled, lightly crushed
1 onion (any kind), not peeled, quartered
2 Tbsp extra-virgin olive oil
1 Tbsp white miso (optional)
6 cups water
a handful of herbs (parsley, basil, and/or sage)
salt and black pepper
cooked noodles, to serve (optional)

1 If you can see green shoots at the tops of the garlic or onion, remove and discard them.

2 Heat the oil in a large saucepan over medium-low heat. Add the whole garlic and cook for 5–7 minutes, turning it over in the oil until evenly golden brown all over. Add the onion and miso, if using, and cook for another 5 minutes, stirring occasionally, until the onion is soft.

3 Pour in the water and give everything a good stir to combine. Turn the heat up to bring the broth to a boil, then reduce to a simmer. Stir through the herbs, and leave to simmer for 20–30 minutes, until the broth is fragrant and a deep golden brown. Season with salt and black pepper.

4 Strain the broth and serve hot, with added cooked noodles if you like. Alternatively, leave to cool completely before storing in a sealed container in the fridge for 2 weeks, or freeze in ice cube trays for up to 3 months.

Tips For a deeper, richer umami flavor, add 2 oz mushrooms.

Put the cooked veg in your compost bin if you have one.

 about 1.5 quarts
 5 mins
 35–45 mins
 Up to 2 weeks
 Up to 3 months

Roasted Onion and Leek Dip

This roasted onion dip is a real crowd-pleaser. It's easy to put together and goes well with chips or with crunchy raw veg such as carrots, cauliflower florets, and celery. It is also perfect for spreading in sandwiches and burgers.

2 onions, thinly sliced
1 large leek, thinly sliced, including the green top
4 spring onions, roots removed
3 garlic cloves, chopped
1 Tbsp olive oil
pinch of salt
¼ tsp black pepper
zest and juice of ½ lemon
½ cup mayonnaise
½ cup yogurt (see note on page 16)
1 Tbsp milk (optional)
2 fresh thyme sprigs, chopped
1 Tbsp snipped fresh chives

1 Preheat the oven to 350°F. Line a baking dish with parchment paper.

2 Put the onions, leek, spring onions, and garlic in the baking pan and toss with the olive oil, salt, and pepper. Roast for about 15 minutes, until soft and lightly charred. Remove from the oven and let cool.

3 Add the roasted veg to a food processor and add the lemon juice and zest, mayo, and yogurt. Pulse until the mixture is smooth but slightly chunky. If too thick, add 1 tablespoon of milk to loosen the mixture.

4 Serve in a bowl, sprinkled with thyme and chives.

 8   10 mins   15 mins   Up to 5 days   Up to 1 month   **GF**

7– Non-Dairy

Milk
Yogurt

Fragrant Flatbreads

I love eating with my hands—it's a really fun and playful way to appreciate food in a whole new way. These light, fluffy breads are the perfect vehicle for scooping up leftover sauce or curry—try them with my Easy Spinach and Chickpea Curry on page 159 or the Tofu Butter "Chicken" on page 124.

¼ cup warm water
1 Tbsp maple syrup
1 tsp active dry yeast
¾ cup warm milk (I use oat)
¾ cup yogurt (I use coconut)
2½ cups all-purpose flour, plus more for dusting
1½ tsp baking powder
1 tsp baking soda
¼ tsp salt
½ cup butter, melted (see note on page 16)
2 garlic cloves, grated
1 cup chopped fresh herbs (e.g., basil, parsley, chives, dill)

1 In a large bowl, whisk together the warm water, maple syrup, and yeast. Set aside for 5 minutes, until foamy.

2 Add the milk, yogurt, flour, baking powder, baking soda, and salt to the bowl. Use your hands to combine and bring it together into a sticky dough, making sure the flour is completely incorporated. Dust with a little more flour, then knead the dough and shape into a smooth ball. Cover the bowl with a clean dry kitchen towel and leave in a warm place for 1 hour, until doubled in size.

3 Shape the dough into 8 even balls. On a lightly dusted surface, use a rolling pin to roll out each piece of dough into an oval shape, about 8 inches long and ¼ inch thick.

4 Heat a large frying pan over medium-high heat until very hot. Carefully coat the bottom of the pan with a small amount of melted butter. Place an oval in the pan, then brush its surface with a little more melted butter. Cover the pan with a lid and cook for 1 minute. When the dough has puffed up, gently turn it over and cook, lid off, for 1–2 minutes, until you can see dark spots underneath and the bread is cooked through. Wrap the cooked flatbreads in a clean kitchen towel to keep warm while you cook the rest.

5 Melt the remaining butter with the garlic in a small pan over low heat for 3–5 minutes, stirring until the garlic is lightly browned. Remove from the heat, stir in the herbs, and drizzle over the warm flatbreads to serve.

Tips To make ahead, you can knead the dough and then leave it to proof overnight in the fridge.

Store in an airtight container at room temperature for up to 3 days or in the fridge for up to 7 days.

Leftovers are amazing: reheat in a frying pan with a little oil for about 3 minutes.

 8 breads
 15 mins
 20–30 mins
 Up to 7 days
 Up to 3 months

Best Ever "Buttermilk" Pancakes

As an American, being able to make a stack of light and fluffy pancakes for weekend breakfasts is essential! I've been perfecting this recipe for years. No need to look elsewhere for pancake recipes—this is for sure the best! Top with fruit and drizzle with maple syrup, or turn to page 170 for some alternative topping ideas.

1½ cups oat milk
2 Tbsp apple cider vinegar or lemon juice
1 cup buckwheat flour
¾ cup gluten-free all-purpose flour
zest of 1 lemon
1½ tsp baking powder
1 tsp baking soda
2 tsp sugar
½ tsp salt
1 Tbsp chia seeds (optional)
1 Tbsp vegetable oil, plus more for greasing (optional)

1 To make the "buttermilk," whisk the milk and apple cider vinegar in a bowl until foamy and set aside for 5–10 minutes.

2 In a large bowl, whisk together the flours, lemon zest, baking powder, baking soda, sugar, salt, and chia seeds, if using. Keep whisking, slowly pouring in the mixture and the oil, until the batter is smooth and pourable and the flour is completely incorporated.

3 Heat a non-stick frying pan over medium heat (depending on your pan, you may like to add a little oil to prevent the pancakes from sticking). Once the pan is hot, pour in half-ladlefuls of the batter to make small pancakes. Cook for 1–2 minutes, until the pancakes rise and bubbles appear on the surface. Carefully turn them over and cook on the other side for 1 minute. Keep warm while you cook the remaining batter.

4 To serve, stack the pancakes high and serve with fresh seasonal fruit and maple syrup.

Tips Do not flatten the pancakes with the spatula as they cook: allow them to rise to thick, fluffy pancakes.

Buckwheat flour is naturally gluten-free, but brands vary: if gluten is an issue for you, check the label. You may also need to check the label of the baking powder.

 12 pancakes
 10 mins
 10–15 mins
 3 days
 Up to 1 month
GF

Cinnamon and Chocolate Churros

When I was living in New York, every day outside the subway station in Brooklyn two women sold the most incredible churros from a shopping cart. Crispy, fried bread coated in cinnamon-and-nutmeg-spiced sugar and dunked in melted chocolate, just like those NY churros, these are made with love and are completely irresistible.

2 cups milk (I use oat)

1 cup + 3 Tbsp sugar

3 Tbsp vegetable oil, plus more for deep frying

1¾ cups gluten-free all-purpose flour

1 tsp baking powder

½ tsp ground ginger

1 Tbsp ground cinnamon

¼ tsp ground nutmeg

5¼ oz dark chocolate, roughly chopped

1   Pour the milk into a medium saucepan over medium heat. Stir in 3 tablespoons of sugar until the sugar has dissolved. Bring to a boil, then immediately remove from the heat, stir in the oil, then stir in the flour, baking powder, and ground ginger until it comes together into a soft dough. Transfer the dough to a piping bag fitted with a small star-shaped nozzle.

2   In a shallow bowl, mix the remaining sugar with the cinnamon and nutmeg.

3   Melt two-thirds of the chocolate in a heatproof bowl set over a pan of barely simmering water, ensuring the bottom of the bowl doesn't touch the water. Stir frequently until the chocolate has completely melted. Add the remaining chocolate, remove the bowl from the heat, and stir until the chocolate is silky smooth.

4   To cook your churros, heat 2–3 inches of vegetable oil in a large, deep, heavy-bottomed pan set over high heat until it reaches 375°F. I use a cook's thermometer to check the temperature. If you don't have a cook's thermometer, carefully drop in a small piece of the dough: it should immediately sizzle and turn golden brown.

5   When the oil is hot enough, carefully pipe 2–3 inch lengths of dough directly into the hot oil—do not overcrowd the pan—and fry for about 1 minute, until golden brown underneath, then gently flip to cook on the other side.

6   Use a slotted spoon or tongs to transfer the cooked churros to some paper towels to remove excess oil. Sprinkle with the spiced sugar and toss to coat. Repeat with the rest of the dough.

7   To serve, dip the hot sugar-coated churros in the melted chocolate.

Tips Check that the baking powder is gluten-free if gluten is an issue for you.

Serve immediately or they will go soft.

 8   15 mins   15 mins   **GF**

Spongy Banana and Chocolate Glazed Doughnuts

Making these doughnuts is probably the best reason I know to use up old ripe bananas! Bananas bring sweetness, flavor, and extra moisture to the dough, while a dark chocolate glaze provides a sophisticated finish. If you don't know about doughnut holes, be prepared to meet your new favorite bite-sized treat!

2½ tsp active dry yeast
¼ cup plus ¼ tsp granulated sugar
¼ cup lukewarm water
¾ cup oat milk, or other non-dairy alternative
1 ripe banana, peeled and mashed
5 Tbsp butter, melted and cooled (see note on page 16)
1 tsp vanilla extract
½ tsp salt
3¾ cups all-purpose flour, plus more for dusting
vegetable oil, for frying, plus ½ tsp

Chocolate glaze
5¼ oz dark chocolate, roughly chopped

Optional toppings
crushed walnuts
toasted shredded coconut

Tips Don't crowd the pan or the temperature of the oil will drop.

Drizzle the chocolate glaze over the doughnuts or dunk them in to coat them on one side.

If there's any leftover chocolate, save it or drizzle it over anything you like.

Best served hot!

1 In a small bowl, whisk the yeast, ¼ teaspoon granulated sugar, and warm water. Once foamy, let it stand for about 5 minutes.

2 Meanwhile, in a large bowl, combine the oat milk, mashed banana, butter, vanilla extract, salt, and remaining granulated sugar. Add the yeast mixture and stir well.

3 Add ⅓ cup flour at a time to the wet mixture, mixing well with a dough whisk or wooden spoon, until no streaks of flour can be seen before adding more flour. With floured hands, place the dough on a floured surface and knead lightly to form a ball. Place the ball of dough in a large bowl, and drizzle ½ teaspoon oil around the inside of the bowl. Cover with a damp clean kitchen towel and keep in a warm, controlled environment, like the inside of an oven, for about 1½ hours, until doubled in size.

4 Transfer the risen dough to a floured surface and lightly sprinkle with flour. With a rolling pin, gently roll the dough into a 14 x 25-inch rectangle. The rectangle should be 1 inch thick. With a doughnut cutter or a 1¼-inch round cutter and a ½-inch cutter for the holes, cut out rounds as close together as possible. Gather the leftover scraps of dough, reroll, and cut again. Repeat until there's no dough remaining.

Continued →

 Makes 12–14 doughnuts, plus doughnut holes
 30 mins
 20 mins
 Up to 3 days
Up to 3 months

Continued $\rightarrow$

5 Place the doughnuts and doughnut holes on a tray lined with parchment paper, making sure there's space between them to rise. Cover lightly with plastic wrap and let them rise somewhere warm for 30–45 minutes until puffed up.

6 Pour the vegetable oil into a large wide, heavy-bottomed pan to a depth of about 2 inches. Heat over medium-high heat to 375°F—test it with a kitchen thermometer or drop in a small cube of bread; it should sizzle and turn brown in about 15 seconds. Meanwhile, line 2 wire racks with paper towels.

7 Carefully lower a few doughnuts and holes into the hot oil, making sure to not crowd the pan. Fry for about 2 minutes, until golden brown underneath. Carefully flip them over once and fry for 1–2 minutes. The doughnut holes will take less time to cook, so keep a closer eye on them. Remove with a skimmer or slotted spoon and place on the wire racks to cool.

8 Place two-thirds of the chocolate in a heatproof bowl that fits over a saucepan. Bring about 1 inch water to a simmer over medium-high heat. Set the bowl over the saucepan, making sure the bottom of the bowl doesn't touch the hot water. Reduce the heat, and melt the chocolate, stirring frequently. Once the chocolate has completely melted, add the remaining chocolate to the bowl, remove from heat, and let it cool slightly, continuing to stir until the chocolate is silky smooth.

9 Once the chocolate is slightly cooled, scoop some chocolate onto a spoon and drizzle the chocolate over the tops of the doughnut rings, creating a pattern of your liking. Dip the doughnut holes in the chocolate glaze and return to the rack.

10 Sprinkle over any additional toppings while the chocolate is still slightly wet and glossy. Let the doughnuts and holes stand until the glaze sets.

Blackberry Shortbread Frozen Yogurt

I've been trying to find a frozen yogurt recipe that has the perfect creamy consistency but that's also quite quick to make—and this is it! It's sweet and smooth, with buttery, crunchy cookies folded in for contrasting textures. Freeze-dried berries on top add extra color and sweetness.

3⅓ cups blackberries
1⅔ cups yogurt (see note on page 16)
½ of a 14-oz can sweetened condensed milk
⅓ cup maple syrup
2 tsp vanilla extract
1 cup minus 1 Tbsp cream
zest and juice of 1 lemon
5 oz shortbread cookies or cookies, crushed and chilled in the fridge
4 Tbsp freeze-dried strawberries or raspberries

1 In a food processor, blend half the blackberries with the yogurt, condensed milk, maple syrup, and vanilla extract until smooth and creamy.

2 Pour the cream and lemon juice into a large bowl and, with a hand mixer, lightly whip for about 5 minutes until it's increased in size and bubbly. Stir in the blackberry mixture and lemon zest until combined. Pour the mixture into a freezer-proof container and cover with a lid or plastic wrap. Freeze for 1 hour.

3 After 1 hour, remove from the freezer and whisk until smooth. Fold in the remaining blackberries and shortbread cookies. Scatter the freeze-dried fruit on top and cover. Freeze for another hour, or overnight.

4 Remove from the freezer to soften a little before serving. Run an ice cream scoop or large spoon under hot water, wipe clean, and scoop.

Tips Blackberries are the hero here, but you can swap them out for strawberries, blueberries, or raspberries.

The water content of each berry may vary. Sometimes I like to press the fruit through a sieve, capturing the liquid and freezing it for smoothies and cocktails. Keep the fruit pulp and continue with the recipe. More water content means the end product will have shards of ice throughout.

You can substitute orange juice for the lemon.

Try folding in ground cardamom or a drizzle of balsamic vinegar in step 3.

 8

 10 mins

Freeze time: 2 hours or overnight

 Up to 3 months

Fluffy Scones

There's not much better than filling your home with the smell of baking. Allow these light and airy scones to cool a little before topping with a generous dollop of jam and thick cream. The only question is: Which one goes on first? Definitely cream first, then the jam, right?

⅔ cup milk (I use oat)
1 tsp vanilla extract
1 Tbsp lemon juice and zest of 1 lemon
2¼ cups self-rising flour, plus more for dusting
1 tsp baking powder
6½ Tbsp butter, cold and cubed (see note on page 16)
¼ cup sugar

To serve
strawberry jam
clotted cream

1 Heat the milk in a pan over low heat until lukewarm—keep an eye on it as you don't want it to get too hot. Remove from the heat and stir in the vanilla and lemon juice. Set aside to cool.

2 Preheat the oven to 425°F. Line a baking sheet with parchment paper.

3 Sift the flour and baking powder into a large bowl. Add the butter and use your fingertips to lightly rub everything together until it looks like fine crumbs. Stir in the sugar and lemon zest.

4 Reserving 2 tablespoons of the milk mixture for brushing on top of your scones, pour the rest into the flour mixture and lightly knead for about 2 minutes, until you have a shaggy, slightly sticky dough. On a lightly floured surface, use your fingertips to gently press out the dough until it is about 1¼ inches thick. Using a 3-inch round cutter, cut out the scones and place them on the lined baking sheet. Gather the leftover dough, reroll, and cut out more scones. You should get 8 or 9.

5 Lightly brush the scones with the reserved milk mixture and bake for 15–20 minutes, until well risen and golden brown. Remove from the oven and leave to cool on a wire rack.

6 Split the scones and serve with strawberry jam and cream.

Tips Don't overhandle the dough, and don't roll it out too thinly or you won't have deep, fluffy scones.

Store leftovers in an airtight container at room temperature for up to 3 days or in the fridge for up to 5 days.

 8 or 9 scones
 20 mins
 15–20 mins
 Up to 5 days
 Up to 1 month

No-Waste Cereal Milk Ice Cream

This is based on the incredible breakfast-meets-dessert treat created by the amazing Momofuku Milk Bar in New York. When I first tried it more than ten years ago, it blew my mind. As a kid, drinking that sweetened milk at the bottom of the cereal bowl was always the best bit, and here is the adult version turned into ice cream!

3 cups cornflakes, or any cereal
1 (14-oz) can full-fat coconut milk
1 cup milk (I use oat)
1 tsp ground cinnamon
1 tsp vanilla extract
¼ cup sweetened condensed coconut milk
2 Tbsp sugar
1 tsp olive oil
sea salt

1 Preheat the oven to 300ºF. Line a baking sheet with parchment paper.

2 Spread the cornflakes evenly over the baking sheet and bake for 10–15 minutes, until lightly browned. Remove from the oven and leave to cool.

3 In a pan over low heat, gently stir the coconut milk and oat milk, ensuring that any solid coconut has melted. Leave to cool for 10 minutes.

4 Transfer the toasted cornflakes to a large bowl and pour in the cooled coconut and oat milk, cinnamon, and vanilla; stir well to combine. Leave to infuse for 30 minutes.

5 Strain the mixture through a fine sieve into another large bowl. Gently press as much milk as you can from the cornflakes: if small bits of cereal fall into the milk, this is fine. Place the used cornflakes in a small container, seal with a lid, and place in the fridge.

6 Whisk the infused milk with the condensed coconut milk, half the sugar, and a pinch of sea salt until well combined. Transfer the mixture to a freezer-proof container with a lid, seal, and freeze overnight, until solid.

7 Shortly before serving, preheat the oven to 350°F and line a baking sheet with parchment paper.

8 In a bowl, combine the used cornflakes with the olive oil and the remaining sugar. Spread the mixture evenly on the lined baking sheet and bake for 12–15 minutes until golden and lightly crispy. Remove from the oven and leave to cool. Lightly crush to break up into small clusters.

9 Remove the ice cream from the freezer and serve immediately, in a bowl, cup, or cone, topped with the cornflake clusters and a pinch of salt.

 6   15 mins   25–30 mins   Up to 3 months

Salted Chocolate, Peanut Butter, and Tahini Brownies

Have you ever seen a more psychedelic, magical brownie?!

2 Tbsp flaxseed meal
1¼ cups all-purpose flour
¾ cup unsweetened cocoa powder
2 tsp baking powder
¾ cup brown sugar
¼ tsp sea salt, plus more for finishing
1¾ cups dark chocolate chips
½ tsp instant coffee powder
1 cup oat milk
½ cup butter, melted (see note on
  page 16)
1 tsp vanilla extract
¼ cup smooth peanut butter
1 Tbsp tahini

1 Preheat the oven to 400°F. Line a 9-inch square baking dish with parchment paper.

2 In a small bowl, combine the flaxseed with 3 tablespoons of water. Set aside for 5–10 minutes until it thickens and develops a jelly-like consistency.

3 Into a large bowl, sift the flour, cocoa powder, and baking powder. Stir in the sugar and salt.

4 Place a heatproof bowl over a saucepan of simmering water, making sure the bottom of the bowl doesn't touch the hot water. Weigh out and set aside ½ cup of the chocolate. Melt two-thirds of the remaining chocolate in the heatproof bowl, stirring often. Once completely melted, add the remaining one-third of the chocolate and the instant coffee powder, remove from heat, and stir until silky smooth. Leave to cool for 5 minutes.

5 Fold the melted chocolate, oat milk, butter, flaxseed paste, and vanilla extract into the dry ingredients until well combined. Pour the mixture into the lined baking pan. Tap gently against the counter to remove any trapped air bubbles.

6 Bake for 25 minutes; the top should be slightly cracked and cooked whereas the inside should be slightly gooey. Remove from the oven and allow to cool completely in the pan.

7 Set a heatproof bowl over a pan of simmering water, making sure it doesn't touch the water. Melt two-thirds of the remaining chocolate in the bowl, stirring. Once melted, add the rest of it, remove from the heat, and stir until smooth. Cool for 5 minutes.

8 Spread the remaining chocolate mixture over the brownies, then top with dollops of peanut butter and tahini. Using a knife or a toothpick, gently swirl the peanut butter and tahini together to create a magical design. Transfer the brownies to the fridge to cool for about 45 minutes.

9 Cut the chilled brownies, sprinkle with sea salt, and serve.

 12

 10 mins

 1 hour

Up to 3 days at room temperature; 7 days in the fridge

 Up to 1 month

8– Fruits

Apple
Banana
Berries
Citrus

Lemon and Poppy Seed Shortbread Fingers with Lemon Glaze

I can't resist a lemon-flavored cookie or cake. Don't get me started on lemon drizzle . . . In these buttery, crumbly shortbread fingers, poppy seeds provide extra crunch and a subtle flavor that goes really well with citrus fruits. A sweet lemon glaze brings everything together. Perfect with a cup of tea. Or with ice cream. Or with yogurt for breakfast. There are no rules to eating these!

1 cup plus 6 Tbsp very cold butter (see note on page 16)

½ cup granulated sugar

zest of 3 lemons and juice of 1 lemon (save the remaining lemons to make my Citrus Cubes on page 252)

1 Tbsp poppy seeds, plus more for decorating

1 tsp vanilla extract

2¼ cups all-purpose flour

pinch of salt

1 cup confectioners' sugar

1 Preheat the oven to 350°F. Line an 8 x 12-inch baking dish with parchment paper.

2 Put the cold butter in an electric mixer bowl with the sugar and whip until light and fluffy. Whip in the lemon zest, poppy seeds, and the vanilla extract.

3 Fold in the flour along with a pinch of salt, then tip the mixture into the prepared pan and press down a little. Use a knife to score about 20 rectangles, not cutting all the way through—this makes the shortbread fingers easier to cut after baking.

4 Bake for 30 minutes, until lightly golden. Allow to cool, then cut and place on a wire rack over a plate.

5 In a small bowl, mix the confectioners' sugar with the juice of half a lemon and stir well. Add as much of the other half of the lemon juice as you need to make a thick-drizzle icing. Drizzle the lemony glaze over the shortbread, then sprinkle with poppy seeds and leave to set.

Tip Try substituting the lemon for lime, orange, or grapefruit.

 20 fingers   10 mins   30 mins   Up to 2 weeks   Up to 1 month

Blueberry Ginger Galette

The more rustic this looks, the better. Don't stress about folding the pastry perfectly, just enjoy the process. Easy to make, this fruity dessert is really beautiful and sure to win over any crowd. It just needs a scoop of ice cream before serving.

1⅔ cups all-purpose flour, plus more for dusting
2 Tbsp sugar
1 tsp salt
½ cup cold butter, cubed (see note on page 16)
2 Tbsp cold water
1 tsp lemon juice
2 tsp milk (I use oat)

Blueberry filling
1 pint fresh blueberries
1 tsp grated fresh ginger, or 1 Tbsp ground ginger
zest of 1 lemon and juice of ½ lemon
¼ cup sugar
2 tsp cornstarch

1 In a food processor, combine the flour, sugar, and salt, then add the butter and pulse until the mixture looks like fine crumbs. Tip the mixture into a large bowl, add the cold water and lemon juice, and work with your hands to combine until the mixture forms a ball of dough.

2 Tip the dough out onto a floured surface and shape to form a disc. Place on a large plate, cover with a clean kitchen towel, and chill for at least 1 hour, or up to 48 hours.

3 Meanwhile, put the blueberries into the same large bowl with the ginger, lemon juice and zest, sugar, and cornstarch. Stir to combine, then chill until you're ready to roll the pastry.

4 Preheat the oven to 350°F.

5 Remove the dough from the fridge and place it on a lightly floured sheet of parchment paper. Cover with another sheet of parchment. Gently roll the dough in every direction until you have a 12-inch round (don't worry if it's not a perfect circle). Transfer the dough to a baking sheet and lift off the top sheet of parchment.

6 Spoon the blueberry mix into the center of the pastry (leave the wet sugary mixture in the bowl), leaving about 2 inches around the edges. Gently lift the edges and fold them up and over the blueberry mixture, slightly overlapping the pastry as you go. Leave a blueberry window in the center. Gently brush the edges of the pastry with the milk mixed with 1 teaspoon of the remaining blueberry sugar mixture.

7 Bake for about 35 minutes, until the pastry is golden brown and the blueberry mixture is bubbling. Remove from the oven and leave to cool slightly before cutting and serving.

8 Serve with ice cream; try my cereal milk ice cream (page 218), but don't get confused—this isn't breakfast.

Tip You want to make sure the pastry has chilled enough before you roll it and spoon over the blueberry mixture.

 8   15 mins   35 mins   Up to 7 days   Up to 1 month

Passion Fruit and Mango Aquafaba Meringues

Fresh fruit and meringues are always a winning combination. Aquafaba is such an amazing ingredient; from pasta (on page 240) to my chocolate cake on page 250, it's so incredibly versatile. Here, it's whipped into a cloud and baked into a crunchy, crispy, perfectly chewy meringue that melts in your mouth. I like the sharp-sweet contrast of the passion fruit and mango, but you can also swap the tropical fruit for strawberries, blueberries, raspberries, or bananas.

1½ cups heavy cream (see note on
   page 16)
1¼ cups coconut yogurt
2 mangoes
1 passion fruit
1 kiwi, thinly sliced with the skin on

Meringue
⅔ cup aquafaba
⅔ cup sugar

To serve
¾ cup toasted shredded coconut
6 fresh mint leaves
zest of 1 lime

1   Preheat the oven to 250°F. Line a baking sheet with parchment paper.

2   If you don't already have some aquafaba, drain a 14-oz can of chickpeas and measure out the reserved liquid. Tip the liquid into a large bowl (if you have a stand mixer or electric whisk, you can save yourself the arm work!) and whisk for 15–18 minutes, adding 1–2 tablespoons of sugar every minute, until it reaches stiff peaks and the mixture is glossy and thick. (You know it's ready when you can flip the bowl over your head and nothing happens!)

3   Spoon big tablespoons of the aqaufaba mix onto the lined baking sheet; you should make about 12 large meringues. Bake for 2 hours, then turn off the oven and leave them in the oven to cool for 45 minutes. Do not open the oven door.

4   In a bowl, lightly whip the cream for about 2 minutes, until slightly thickened, then fold in the yogurt. Slice the mangoes and scoop out the flesh of each. Blend the flesh from 1 mango in a high-speed blender to make a purée, and transfer to a bowl. Cut the passion fruit in half and spoon the pulp into the blended mango. Dice the remaining mango.

5   To serve, chop half of the meringues into big chunks and fold them through the cream and yogurt mixture. Swirl in the mango and passion fruit purée. Press 1 slice of kiwi on the inside of each jar, then spoon the meringue mixture into each jar. Top with the mango chunks and toasted coconut flakes. Crush a little more meringue and scatter on top—you might not need all the meringues! Finish with the fresh mint and lime zest.

Tip If you have leftover meringues, store in a sealed and lined container at room temperature for 1 week or up to 1 month in the freezer.

 6   25 mins   2 hours   Up to 7 days   Up to 1 month   **GF**

Strawberry Granita with Lemon Cream

Each spoonful of this summer dessert is like a dance in your mouth between the sweet crunch from the strawberry ice, the zingy citrus cream, and the crumbly shortbread pieces. Eat it in a bowl or cone—or straight from the tub. I'm not here to judge.

2 cups plus 2 Tbsp water
1 cup sugar
2½ cups strawberries
1 tsp vanilla extract
zest and juice of 1 lemon
1 cup heavy cream (see note on page 16)
2 Tbsp confectioners' sugar
shortbread, to serve (see my Lemon and Poppy Seed Shortbread on page 224)

1 Start by pouring the water and sugar into a large saucepan. Place over a medium heat, stirring occasionally for about 2 minutes, until the sugar has dissolved.

2 Process the strawberries, including the leaves, in a high-speed blender to make a purée.

3 Remove the saucepan from the heat and add the strawberry purée, vanilla extract, and lemon juice. Stir well, then pour the mixture into a baking pan and slide into the freezer. Every 45 minutes for the next 5–6 hours, remove the pan and use a fork to scrape and break up the ice crystals—you'll be left with a perfect granita!

4 When you're ready to serve, lightly whip the cream, lemon zest, and confectioners' sugar. Spoon the granita into bowls or glasses, top with the lemon cream, and serve with shortbread.

Tip Strawberry leaves are edible, but totally optional.

 6
 10 mins
 2 mins
 Up to 3 months

Chocolate Orange Peanut Cheesecake

Beautifully rich and chocolatey, candied orange takes this cheesecake to another dimension! It has a peanut and digestive biscuit base, coconut cream filling, and a chocolate orange topping. With layers of flavor and texture in every slice, it's a total showstopper!

Chocolate peanut base
10 oz gluten-free digestive biscuits
2 Tbsp cocoa powder
½ cup peanuts, chopped
5 Tbsp butter, melted and cooled to room temperature (see note on page 16)
1 Tbsp smooth peanut butter

Orange cheesecake
1⅓ lb cream cheese (see note on page 16)
zest of 2 oranges
1 cup full-fat coconut cream
1½ cups confectioners' sugar
1 tsp vanilla extract

Chocolate ganache topping
1 cup full-fat coconut cream
7 oz dark chocolate, roughly chopped
zest of 1 orange

Candied orange and peanut topping
sliced oranges (from above)
1 cup sugar
7 Tbsp water

To serve
3 Tbsp roasted peanuts, roughly chopped
1 Tbsp shavings of dark chocolate
any reserved orange zest

1 Start by making the chocolate peanut base. Process the digestives to a fine crumble in a food processor and tip into a bowl. Stir together the rest of the ingredients, then use a spoon to press into the bottom of a 9-inch springform pan.

2 Next make the orange cheesecake layer: whisk the cream cheese with the zest from the oranges, the coconut cream, confectioners' sugar, and vanilla extract. Pour the mixture into the crust in the pan and chill in the fridge to set for 4–5 hours, or overnight.

3 For the chocolate ganache topping, heat the coconut cream over medium heat until bubbling. Remove from the heat and pour over the chocolate in a bowl. Allow to sit for 2 minutes before whisking together. Stir in the orange zest. Cool until you can touch it, then pour over the set cheesecake and put back in the fridge.

4 Slice the zested oranges as finely as you can, ideally ¹⁄₁₆ inch thick. Add the sugar to a large frying pan with the water, and bring to a boil, stirring until the sugar has dissolved. Add the orange slices, turn the heat down to a simmer, and cook for 5–10 minutes, until softened and translucent. Take off the heat and allow to cool in the syrup. Use tongs to move the cool candied orange wheels to a plate lined with parchment paper or a wire rack. (You can store the candied orange slices for 3–4 weeks, in their syrup, in a jar in the fridge.)

5 Lay the slices on the top of the cheesecake, overlapping them so they fit the shape evenly. Place the cheesecake back in the fridge for another 30–45 minutes to chill.

6 To serve, slice the cheesecake and scatter with the roasted crushed peanuts, shaved chocolate, and orange zest.

 8–10 45 mins 15 mins Up to 1 week Up to 1 month *Just potatoes **GF**

Sticky Apple Toffee Pudding

The warm, spiced cake, the sweet and sticky caramel sauce . . . since moving to the UK, I've become a big fan of sticky toffee pudding! Why not elevate yours by adding apples? I always serve mine with a scoop of ice cream for that irresistible hot-cold contrast.

butter, for greasing (see note on page 16)
10 oz pitted Medjool dates
2½ Tbsp flaxseed meal
1 cup oat milk
1 tsp baking soda
5 Tbsp water
2 cups self-rising flour
1 cup sunflower oil
2 Tbsp maple syrup
¾ cup light brown sugar
1 tsp ground cinnamon
pinch of salt
3 apples or pears (or a mixture), cored and cut into ⅜-inch cubes
ice cream or cream, to serve

Sauce
7 Tbsp butter
1 cup dark brown sugar
1 Tbsp maple syrup
7 Tbsp heavy cream

1 Preheat the oven to 350°F. Line a 9 x 13-inch cake pan with parchment paper and lightly grease with butter.

2 Put the dates, flaxseed, oat milk, baking soda, and water in a saucepan over medium heat. Cook for 5 minutes, stirring occasionally, until the dates are softened. Remove from heat and allow to cool for 10 minutes.

3 Sift the flour into a large bowl, then add the sunflower oil, syrup, sugar, cinnamon, a pinch of salt, and the date mixture. Stir until combined; the batter should be quite thick.

4 Add the cubed fruit, stir to combine, then pour into the prepared pan and bake for 40–45 minutes. To check that it's cooked, insert a fork into the middle; it should come out clean.

5 Meanwhile, make the sauce. Melt the butter in a small saucepan over medium heat. Add the sugar and syrup, stirring slowly and continuously until the sugar has dissolved. When the sugar has completely dissolved, slowly pour in the cream while stirring until combined and the sauce is slightly thick and shiny. Set aside ready to be reheated on low heat when you want to serve.

6 Remove the pudding from the oven and allow it to cool for 10–15 minutes. Serve with ice cream or cream and drizzled with the sweet buttery sauce.

 8

 20 mins

 45–50 mins

 Up to 1 week

 Up to 3 months* *Pudding only

Spiced Apple Fritters

There are few things in life that are as delicious or as comforting as a warm homemade dessert, like these fried nuggets of cinnamon-flavored batter stuffed with juicy apple chunks and covered with a lemony drizzle. You can have these scrumptious spiced apple fritters in your hands in less than an hour.

2 large cooking apples, cored and cubed
2 Tbsp lemon juice
2 Tbsp ground flaxseed
4 Tbsp water
3 Tbsp butter, melted (see note on page 16)
½ cup milk (I use oat)
1½ cups all-purpose flour
2 tsp baking powder
1 tsp ground cinnamon
½ tsp ground nutmeg
¼ tsp ground ginger
pinch of ground cardamom
½ tsp sea salt
3 Tbsp sugar
1 Tbsp lemon zest
vegetable oil, for deep frying
1½ cups confectioners' sugar

1   Toss the apples in a bowl with the lemon juice to stop them from browning. Set aside.

2   In a bowl, combine the flaxseed and water, whisk together, and set aside for about 5–10 minutes until it thickens. Stir in the melted butter and milk until combined.

3   Sift the flour, baking powder, spices, and salt into a large bowl. Add the sugar and lemon zest, then pour in the wet mixture and stir well to create a thick batter. Add the apples to the batter, reserving the lemon juice. Mix to combine, then place the batter in the fridge for 20–30 minutes.

4   Pour 2–3 inches of vegetable oil into a large, wide pan and place over medium-high heat until the oil reaches 365°F. I use a cook's thermometer to check the temperature; if you don't have one, carefully drop in a small amount of batter: it should immediately sizzle and turn golden brown.

5   Once the oil is hot, add the batter, a heaping tablespoon at a time; do not crowd the pan. Fry undisturbed for 1–2 minutes, then carefully flip and fry the other side until golden brown. Using a slotted spoon, transfer to a wire rack to drain. Repeat until all the batter is cooked. Leave the fritters to cool for 10–15 minutes.

6   Meanwhile, in a bowl, whisk the confectioners' sugar with the reserved lemon juice until it's slightly thickened and glossy. Pour over the fritters; leave to set for a few minutes before serving.

Tips Any apple (or pear) will work just fine.

Don't make the fritters too big, or the middle may not cook through.

 12–14 fritters   20 mins   15 mins   Up to 5 days   Up to 1 month

Banoffee Moon Pies

Moon pies are such a nostalgic recipe for me. Down the street from my school was a bakery that produced cakes, cookies, doughnuts, and moon pies in a giant warehouse to sell across the US. You could smell the melting sugar in the air. In these grown-up versions, crumbly peanut cookies sandwich sticky marshmallow and banana, then they are coated in chocolate. You'll start with a full moon, then quickly have a total lunar eclipse when you eat the whole thing.

10 oz dark chocolate
2 ripe bananas (save the peel to make my BLT on page 241)

Peanut butter cookies
7 Tbsp butter (see note on page 16)
3 Tbsp smooth peanut butter
6 Tbsp sugar
2¼ cups all-purpose flour, plus more for dusting
pinch of salt
3–4 Tbsp cold milk, if needed (I use oat milk)

Marshmallow fluff
⅔ cup aquafaba
1 tsp cream of tartar
¾ cup sugar
2 tsp vanilla extract

1 Add the butter and peanut butter to a stand mixer with a paddle attachment (or you can do this by hand or use a hand whisk). Beat until light and fluffy. Add the sugar and beat again until creamy and light. Stir in the flour along with a pinch of salt. If the batter is too thick and floury, add 1 tablespoon of cold milk at a time to loosen it.

2 Lay a piece of plastic wrap or parchment paper along your work surface, tip the mixture onto the plastic, and bring together. Wrap in a big flat disc, and place in the fridge to chill and firm up for 1 hour.

3 Preheat the oven to 350°F. Line a baking sheet with parchment paper.

4 Lightly flour a surface and roll out the dough to ⅛-inch thickness. Use a small glass or a cookie cutter to cut out cookies from the dough. Use a spatula or palette knife to lift the cookies onto the lined baking sheet. Combine any leftover dough and repeat until there's no dough left.

5 Bake for 10–12 minutes, until golden brown (you may have to do this in batches or over a couple of sheets). Cool on a wire rack. If the cookies are soft, allow to cool on the baking sheet before transferring.

 20 moon pies
 45 mins
 10–12 mins
 Up to 1 week
Up to 1 month

6   While they are cooling, make the marshmallow fluff. Drain the chickpeas (use the chickpeas for my Curried Pumpkin and Chickpeas on page 120). Measure out the liquid and tip into the bowl of a stand mixer with the whisk attachment (or use a hand whisk). Add the cream of tartar and whisk until stiff peaks form, then add the sugar a spoonful at a time, continuing to whisk for about 15 minutes, until thick and glossy. Add the vanilla extract and give it a final whisk, then transfer to a piping bag if you have one. Keep in the fridge to cool.

7   Melt two-thirds of the chocolate in a heatproof bowl set over a pan of simmering water. Make sure the bottom of the bowl doesn't touch the hot water. Add the remaining one-third of chocolate and stir until smooth and shiny.

8   Assembly time! Pipe the marshmallow fluff over half of the cookies on the rack, using around 1–2 teaspoons on each. Slice the bananas and place on top of the marshmallow fluff. Top with the other half of the cookies to create little sandwiches. Dip the cookie sandwiches in the melted chocolate so they're well coated. Set aside on a wire rack before placing in the fridge to set the chocolate.

9– Leftovers

Fresh No-Egg Pasta

This pasta is made without eggs: it uses aquafaba from a can of chickpeas. I make this recipe every Friday night (pasta night!), so if it's Friday night for you, let's make it together!

¾ cup 00 flour, plus more for dusting
3 Tbsp aquafaba
⅛ tsp ground turmeric

1 Pour the flour onto a clean worktop, and create a small well in the middle. Add the aquafaba and turmeric to the well. Using your fingers, combine them into the flour until you have a shaggy ball of dough. Knead for 5–10 minutes, until the dough is smooth.

2 Alternatively, add the flour and turmeric to a stand mixer; on a low speed, pour in the aquafaba and mix until you have a rough ball of dough. Tip out onto a floured worktop and knead for 5–10 minutes until the dough is smooth.

3 Wrap the dough in plastic wrap or parchment paper and set aside for 15 minutes. This will help the pasta stretch.

4 When you're ready to roll, lightly flour the dough as needed. Pass the dough through a pasta machine, starting at its widest setting. Decrease the setting by one notch and pass the dough through again. Repeat, passing the dough through each setting once.

5 Alternatively, gently roll the dough with a long rolling pin. Lightly flour the dough when needed.

6 To make spaghetti or tagliatelle, cut the pasta with a long, sharp knife or pass it through the machine on the cutting setting. Gather the pasta and place it on a baking sheet; leave to rest for 5 minutes.

7 Bring a large pan of salted water to a boil, add the pasta and cook, stirring occasionally, for about 2 minutes. Strain the pasta and serve with my Simplest Tomato Sauce (page 87).

Tips If making 2 or more portions, you will need to divide the dough, working with 1 portion at a time. Keep any unrolled dough under a clean damp kitchen towel to prevent it from drying out.

Instead of aquafaba from chickpeas, use the liquid from a can of cannellini or red kidney beans.

Use a pasta maker for perfectly rolled pasta dough.

Great for making ravioli, spaghetti, or wider noodles.

Make ahead: keep the dough wrapped in the fridge for up to 2 days.

 1   25 mins   2 mins   Up to 3 days   Up to 1 month

BLT

The B stands for banana peel! Now, I'm not going to force you to eat banana skins, but if there was ever a time to try them, this would be that moment. Bananas are one of the most-wasted fruits in the world. In the UK, over 1 million bananas go to waste every day. Don't slip on this recipe. Crispy, smoky banana peels are my winner over bacon, any day!

4 ripe bananas
2 Tbsp soy sauce or tamari
2 tsp brown sugar
1 tsp smoked paprika
½ tsp garlic powder
½ tsp liquid smoke (optional)
1 Tbsp vegetable oil
4 slices white bread, toasted
8 lettuce leaves
2 heirloom tomatoes, sliced ¼ inch
  thick

Maple miso mustard
2 Tbsp mustard
2 tsp maple syrup
1 tsp miso
¼ tsp cayenne pepper
salt

Lemon-herb mayonnaise
4 Tbsp mayonnaise
1 small garlic clove, finely grated
1 Tbsp lemon juice
1 tsp lemon zest
2 Tbsp chopped mixed fresh herbs
  (e.g., basil, parsley, chives, dill)
salt and black pepper

1 Wash the bananas very well. Remove the peel, and slice the banana and keep in the freezer for a smoothie later. Cut both ends off the peel. Using a spoon, scrape off the fleshy part inside, then cut each piece into 3 strips.

2 In a shallow bowl, whisk together the soy sauce, brown sugar, smoked paprika, garlic powder, and liquid smoke, if using. Add the banana peels, turn to coat in the marinade, and leave for about 15 minutes.

3 Preheat the oven to 375°F. Line a baking sheet with parchment paper.

4 Heat the oil in a large non-stick frying pan over medium heat. Add a few slices of the marinated peels, outer side down first. Cook for 1–2 minutes until crispy around the edges, then flip and cook the other side for 1–2 minutes. Transfer to the lined baking sheet. Repeat until you have fried all the banana peels.

5 Brush with the remaining marinade, then cook in the oven for 5–6 minutes, flipping halfway, until crispy. Transfer to a wire rack to cool slightly.

6 Meanwhile, make the maple miso mustard. Whisk the mustard with the maple syrup, miso, cayenne, and a pinch of salt until combined. Set aside.

7 For the lemon-herb mayonnaise, stir together the mayonnaise, garlic, lemon juice and zest, mixed herbs, and a pinch of salt and black pepper.

8 To serve, spread 2 pieces of toast with the lemon-herb mayo and add 4 lettuce leaves to each. Top with the banana "bacon" and the tomato slices. Spread the remaining slices of toast with some maple miso mustard and close the sandwich. Serve immediately.

Tip For a gluten-free version, use tamari and gluten-free bread.

 2   15 mins   10 mins

Best Festive Leftover Sandwich

When the festive season rolls around, I'm thinking about two things: what can be saved as leftovers and how to cook up those leftovers in a creative way. This recipe gives your festive leftovers a crunchy kick. Totally drool-worthy.

4 Tbsp mayonnaise
2 tsp whole-grain mustard
1⅔ cups leftover Buttery Herb Stuffing (page 74)
leftover cooked vegetables (I used roasted carrots and beets)
1 portion of Roast Dinner Tart (page 119) or Nut Roast Cake (page 70)
3 slices bread
1 Tbsp cranberry sauce

1   Preheat the oven to 300°F.

2   Mix the mayonnaise with the mustard and set aside.

3   Warm the leftovers (stuffing, vegetables, nut roast cake/roast dinner tart) in the oven for about 15 minutes.

4   Toast the bread to your desired toastiness. Spread a thin layer of cranberry sauce on 1 slice, and the mustard-mayonnaise on the other 2 slices.

5   Beginning with the first slice of bread with mustard-mayonnaise, add a layer of nut roast cake/roast dinner tart. Add the slice of bread with cranberry sauce and top with the stuffing and veg. Cover with the last slice of bread, mustard-mayo side facing down.

6   Serve immediately, and if there's any leftover gravy, don't be afraid to dip that sandwich in!

Tip Use any leftover cooked veg: beets, Brussels sprouts, carrots, parsnips, roasted potatoes, sweet potatoes . . .

 1   5 mins   15 mins   Up to 5 days   Up to 2 weeks *stuffing only

Leftover Stuffing Stuffed Mushrooms

The holidays are one of the most wasteful times of the year, and so this is a great way to use up any of the super delicious leftover stuffing from page 74. These stuffed mushrooms make the ideal fun appetizer or finger food to carry on the festivities.

20 small chestnut mushrooms
zest and juice of 1 lemon
1 Tbsp butter (see note on page 16)
1 small shallot, finely chopped
3 garlic cloves, finely chopped
¼ tsp dried thyme
small bunch of fresh parsley, leaves and stems chopped separately, plus more leaves to garnish
1 cup leftover Buttery Herb Stuffing (page 74)
1 Tbsp extra-virgin olive oil
salt and black pepper

1 Wipe the mushrooms clean with kitchen paper. Remove the stems, leaving the mushrooms with a hollow center. Roughly chop the stems and set aside.

2 Preheat the oven to 400°F.

3 In a frying pan over medium heat, dry-fry half of the mushroom caps, gill side up, for 2 minutes. Add 1 tablespoon of lemon juice and a generous pinch of black pepper and cook for 1–2 minutes, stirring often but gently, so you don't break the caps. Transfer the caps to a plate and repeat with the second batch of mushrooms, also adding them to the plate.

4 Melt the butter in the frying pan and fry the shallot, garlic, dried thyme, and 2 tablespoons of chopped parsley stems for about 4 minutes, until soft. Add the chopped mushroom stems and the juice of half the lemon and cook for about 5 minutes, stirring often.

5 Put the mushroom stem mixture into a food processor, add the parsley leaves, and process to a purée. Tip the mixture into a bowl and combine with the leftover stuffing. Season to taste with salt and black pepper.

6 Stuff the mushroom caps with the filling and smooth over the tops. Arrange the mushroom caps close together in a baking dish. Drizzle with the extra-virgin olive oil and bake for 10–15 minutes.

7 Best served hot. To serve, garnish each mushroom with a little lemon zest and a parsley leaf.

Tips Fry the mushrooms for just a few minutes to reduce moisture and prevent them from going soggy.

Defrost, then reheat in the oven at 300°F for 10–15 minutes.

 8   20 mins   25–30 mins   Up to 5 days   Up to 2 weeks

Leftover Burger Flatbreads

Leftover burgers never tasted so good. With inspiration from Middle Eastern cooking, these burger balls are fried until crispy and placed on a pile of spicy cucumber and feta salad, with a sweet and tangy tahini sauce. Eat with a fork and knife, or get your hands involved—fold up the flatbread and take a big bite. An easy weeknight dinner or weekend brunch.

4 uncooked burger patties (page 68 or page 131)
2 Tbsp chopped fresh dill, including stems
2 Tbsp chopped fresh parsley, including stems
2 garlic cloves, grated
5 Tbsp vegetable oil
4 flatbreads, warmed
Pickled Red Onion (page 267)
pinch of sumac (optional), to serve

Cucumber salad
1 small cucumber, peeled lengthwise into ribbons
4 cherry tomatoes, chopped
1 tsp chopped fresh dill
¼ tsp ground cumin
¼ tsp smoked paprika
¼ cup crumbled feta (see note on page 16)
1 Tbsp extra-virgin olive oil
juice of ½ lemon

Tahini sauce
5 Tbsp tahini
juice of ½ lemon
1 garlic clove, finely grated
1 tsp maple syrup
1 tsp harissa paste, or to taste

1 In a bowl, combine the uncooked patties with the dill, parsley, and garlic. In the palms of your hands, roll the mixture into about 20 walnut-sized balls. Place on a lined baking sheet and chill for 15 minutes.

2 To make the cucumber salad, put the cucumber in a bowl, add all the remaining ingredients, and toss to combine. Set aside.

3 To make the tahini sauce, put all the ingredients in a small bowl and stir until smooth. If you like things hotter, add more harissa.

4 Heat the vegetable oil in a frying pan over medium-high heat. Once hot, add the burger balls and fry for 5–7 minutes, turning occasionally, until crispy. Drain on paper towels or a wire rack.

5 Add the cucumber salad to the warm flatbreads and top with the burger balls and pickled red onion. Drizzle with the tahini sauce and sprinkle with a pinch of sumac, if you like.

Tip Super-versatile: use any leftover uncooked burger.

 4
 20 mins
 10 mins
 Up to 5 days
 Up to 1 month* *burger only

Leftovers

Coffee Ground Pancakes

A fan favorite, with over 3 million views. The coffee grounds (depending on the variety) offer nutty, chocolatey notes and are quite subtle. Now you can drink and eat your coffee at the same time!

1½ cups self-rising flour
1 tsp baking powder
½ tsp ground cinnamon
1 Tbsp light brown sugar
2–3 Tbsp used coffee grounds
1¼ cups oat milk
2–3 tsp vegetable oil (optional)
salt

To serve
fresh strawberries
chocolate shavings
confectioners' sugar
maple syrup

1 In a large bowl, whisk together the flour, baking powder, cinnamon, sugar, coffee grounds, and a pinch of salt. Keep whisking while you slowly pour in the milk, until you have a thick, pourable batter.

2 Heat a non-stick frying pan over medium heat (depending on your pan, you may like to add a little oil to prevent the pancakes from sticking). Once the pan is hot, add half-ladlefuls of the batter to make small pancakes. Cook for about 2 minutes, until the underside is golden brown and the edges are set and bubbles start to form on the surface. Flip and cook on the other side for 1–2 minutes. Keep warm while you cook the remaining batter.

3 To serve, stack the pancakes and serve with fresh strawberries, chocolate shavings, a dusting of confectioners' sugar, and a drizzle of maple syrup.

Tips You can also use coffee grounds in cookies, muffins, or cakes.

Use gluten-free flour and baking powder if you prefer.

 12 pancakes
 5 mins
 10–15 mins
 Up to 3 days
 Up to 1 month

Triple Chocolate Birthday Cake

You'll be finding ways to use up chickpeas just so you can make this chocolate cake! Aquafaba is whisked until fluffy, then folded into chocolate and flour to produce a beautifully light cake that melts in your mouth.

⅔ cup aquafaba
⅔ cup brown sugar
¾ cup granulated sugar
1 tsp salt
7 Tbsp butter, at room temperature
   (see note on page 16)
3¾ cups all-purpose flour
1 cup cocoa powder
1 tsp baking powder
7 Tbsp milk

Chocolate frosting
7 oz dark chocolate, roughly chopped
1 tsp vanilla extract
6 Tbsp full-fat coconut cream (from the
   top of a can of coconut milk)
2 Tbsp cold butter
1¼ cups confectioners' sugar, plus a
   little more if needed

To serve
chocolate shavings

Tips Be patient, don't rush the steps.

Incorporate fresh or freeze-dried raspberries into this cake.

1   Preheat the oven to 400°F. Line two 8-inch round layer cake pans with parchment paper.

2   In a bowl, with a hand mixer, whisk the aquafaba on high speed for 5 minutes, until foamy. Keep whisking for about 15 minutes, adding 1–2 tablespoons brown sugar every minute until glossy and stiff peaks form.

3   In a separate bowl, mix the granulated sugar, salt, and butter until pale and fluffy. Sift in the flour, cocoa powder, and baking powder, and fold together well. Add the milk and stir to combine. Carefully pour in the aquafaba mixture, making sure not to knock out all the air and fold it in very gently.

4   Divide the cake batter between the prepared pans and bake for 30 minutes. When cooked, allow the cakes to cool in their pans for about 15 minutes. Gently release the cakes from their pans, transfer to a cooling rack, and leave to cool completely.

5   To make the chocolate frosting, melt two-thirds of the chocolate in a heatproof bowl that fits over a saucepan of simmering water, making sure the bottom of the bowl doesn't touch the hot water, stirring occasionally. Once melted, remove from heat, and stir in the remaining one-third of the chocolate. Set aside to cool for 5 minutes.

6   In a stand mixer or by hand, mix the melted chocolate and vanilla extract on low speed, and gradually mix in the coconut cream and butter until smooth.

7   Add the confectioners' sugar about 1–2 tablespoons at a time. The texture should be firm, soft, and spreadable. Chill the frosting in the fridge for 20 minutes.

8   Once chilled, give it a quick stir. If too loose, add 1–2 tablespoons more confectioners' sugar until firm and spreadable.

9   Spread about half the frosting on top of one cake. Stack the second cake on top and spread the remaining frosting on top. Finish with the shaved chocolate.

 8   30 mins   45 mins   1–2 days at room temperature, up to 5 days in the fridge   Up to 1 month

Citrus Cubes

These citrus ice cubes pack a big punch of flavor—a great way to use that last lemon or lime. Add them to a pitcher of water on a hot day for a refreshing lemon-infused drink, or add to iced tea, lemonade, smoothies, or cocktails. Always good to have in the freezer during the warmer months.

1 lemon or lime
1 cup water

1   Soak the fruit in warm salted water, then scrub.

2   Slice the fruit in half and remove the seeds. Place the fruit in a high-speed blender, add the water, and blend on high speed until smooth.

3   Pour the liquid into an ice cube tray and freeze for 4 hours or overnight.

Tip Take your citrus ice cubes to new levels by adding fresh mint leaves before freezing.

10–14
ice cubes

5 mins

Up to
3 months

GF

Lime Tart with Candied Lime Peel

This tart is all about the candied peel! You can use any citrus you like: lemon, lime, orange, blood orange, grapefruit. I love how it uses up the whole fruit with zero waste. The tart has a beautiful crumbly shortbread base with a creamy, zesty filling and a final flourish of sugary crunch on top.

6 Tbsp butter (see note on page 16)

2½ cups gingersnaps or a variety of shortbread cookies

5 limes

10 oz silken tofu

⅔ cup sweetened condensed milk

2 Tbsp cornstarch

4 Tbsp confectioners' sugar

½ cup sugar

3½ Tbsp water

1 cup heavy cream, to serve

1   Preheat the oven to 350°F.

2   Melt the butter in a small saucepan over medium heat. Add the gingersnaps to a food processor, then pour in the melted butter and pulse until combined. Transfer the crumbly mixture to an 8-inch tart pan and press up the sides. Bake for 8–10 minutes while you prep the filling.

3   For the filling, blend the zest and juice of 3 limes with the silken tofu, condensed milk, cornstarch, and 2 tablespoons of the confectioners' sugar until smooth and creamy. Spoon into the tart pan, spread and smooth evenly, and bake for 40–50 minutes, until set and the crust is golden brown. Set aside to cool completely, then refrigerate for 2–3 hours, until the filling is cold and has set.

4   While the tart is cooling, make the candied lime peel. Take the peel from the 2 un-zested limes and thinly slice into strips, or thinly slice the entire limes. Put the sugar and water in a small saucepan over medium heat and stir occasionally until the sugar has dissolved. Bring to a boil, then add the lime peel or slices, cook for 5 minutes, then remove from heat. With tongs, remove the lime peel or slices and lay on a wire rack to cool completely.

5   To serve, whip the cream and remaining confectioners' sugar until thick and glossy. Pile the whipped cream in the middle of the tart leaving a ¾-inch border all the way around. Scatter the candied lime peel into the border, then slice and serve.

Tips If you fancy really showing off, whip up some aquafaba meringue (see the Moon Pies recipe on page 236), mound it on top, and use a blowtorch to caramelize it just before serving.

Freeze for 1 month without the cream and candied peel. Candied peel can keep for up to 2 weeks in an airtight container lined with parchment paper.

 12

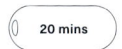 20 mins

55 mins–
1 hour 5 mins

 Up to 1 week

 Up to 1 month

14 Quick Recipe Hacks

Transform and enhance any dish with these flavorful additions.

Roasted Chickpeas

These are great for adding bulk to all kinds of dishes—and they also make an irresistible snack!

1 (14-oz) can chickpeas, drained and rinsed
1 Tbsp olive oil
½ tsp smoked paprika
salt and black pepper

1   Preheat the oven to 425°F. Line a baking sheet with parchment paper.

2   Dry the chickpeas thoroughly on a clean kitchen towel, then toss with the oil, smoked paprika, and a pinch of salt and black pepper.

3   Spread the chickpeas on the lined baking sheet and roast in the oven for 10–15 minutes, tossing halfway, until golden brown and crispy.

Tip Instead of olive oil, for extra flavor use the oil from a jar of sun-dried tomatoes.

Chickpea Mayo

Yes, you can buy ready-made vegan mayo, but even the best brands can't compare with this easy, additive-free, homemade version. Great in sandwiches and burgers, or in dips and dressings.

3 Tbsp aquafaba
1 Tbsp fresh lemon juice
1 tsp apple cider vinegar
1 tsp maple syrup
½ tsp salt
5 Tbsp extra-virgin olive oil

1   In a tall container, add the aquafaba, lemon juice, vinegar, maple syrup, and salt. Using a blender, blend to combine.

2   While blending, slowly stream in the olive oil until the mixture starts to thicken and turn pale and creamy, 1–2 minutes.

3   Keep in a sealed container or jar in the fridge for up to 2 weeks.

Tip For additional flavor, add 1 teaspoon smoked paprika, 1 tablespoon tomato purée, and 1 tablespoon harissa.

Veg Scraps Stock

Save yourself time and money and use peelings and trimmings to make delicious, vibrant veg stock. There's no turning back to using store-bought stock once you start. Use it in soups, such as my Rich Ribollita (page 75), or in any sauce or gravy.

onion scraps
garlic scraps
carrot scraps
celery scraps
herb scraps
mushroom scraps
1 bay leaf
pinch of salt

1 Put your collected scraps in a large saucepan, then add the bay leaf and salt. Pour in enough water to cover the scraps.

2 Bring to a boil, then simmer for at least 10–15 minutes. Simmer longer for more flavor. You'll know it's ready when the vegetables are soft and the liquid turns a slightly darker gold color.

3 Strain over a bowl to collect the stock. Leave to cool before filling containers.

4 Keep in a sealed container in the fridge for up to 7 days or freeze for up to 3 months.

Tips Freeze peels and scraps after cooking your meals. Collect in the freezer until you have enough to make stock: a large handful of scraps will be enough to make about 1 quart of stock.

Add a few peppercorns if you like.

Don't use beet scraps: the color will dominate your soups and sauces.

Don't use cabbage, broccoli, or cauliflower scraps, or the stems of peppers or eggplant, or the stock will taste bitter.

DGS (Delicious Green Sauce)

This versatile, bright, fresh green sauce is perfect tossed with grilled or steamed vegetables or spooned over grilled or pan-fried tofu. Any combination of soft green herbs or bagged salad will work; just be aware the flavor will change a little depending on what you use. Feel free to swap the lemon for lime or garlic for shallot to mix things up.

handful of fresh basil, including the stems
handful of fresh parsley, including the stems
handful of fresh dill
handful of fresh chives
3 garlic cloves
¼ cup yogurt (I use coconut) or sour cream
  (see note on page 16)
zest of 1 lemon
5 Tbsp olive oil
¼ tsp salt

1 In a food processor, process the herbs and garlic to a paste, scraping down the sides of the processor if necessary.

2 Add the yogurt and lemon zest and blend until smooth. With the motor running, stream in the olive oil until evenly combined. Season with the salt.

3 Use immediately or keep in a jar in the fridge for up to 3 days, covered with a thin layer of oil to preserve.

Peanut Sauce

Drizzle over noodles, salads, stir-fried veg, or rice bowls.

2 Tbsp peanut butter, smooth or crunchy
2 Tbsp soy sauce or tamari
3 Tbsp lime juice or rice vinegar
½ tsp red pepper flakes
¼ tsp maple syrup
2 Tbsp water

1 Put all the ingredients (except the water) into a small jar or bowl; close the lid and shake vigorously, or whisk until evenly mixed. If too thick, add a splash of water to loosen.

2 Keep in a covered container in the fridge for up to 2 weeks.

Tip For extra flavor, add 1 grated garlic clove, 1 teaspoon grated fresh ginger, and/or 1 teaspoon toasted sesame seeds.

Everything Seasoning

Sprinkle over avocado toast, hummus, roasted veggies, or baked potatoes.

2 Tbsp poppy seeds
1 Tbsp black sesame seeds
1 Tbsp white sesame seeds
1 Tbsp dried minced garlic
1 Tbsp dried minced onion
1 tsp dried oregano
1 tsp flaky sea salt

1 Put all the ingredients into a jar or container, close the lid, and shake.

2 Store in a cool, dry cupboard for up to 6 months.

Herby Lime Salsa

A zingy salsa to serve with tacos, crisp cucumber salad, roasted veg, Crispy Smashed Potatoes (page 36), or a tofu noodle bowl such as Sticky Broccoli and Crispy Tofu (page 145).

zest of 3 limes
2 Tbsp lime juice
2 garlic cloves, roughly chopped
1 Tbsp grated fresh ginger
¼ cup fresh basil, including stems
¼ cup fresh cilantro, including stems
2 Tbsp fresh mint leaves
¼ cup olive oil
1 tsp salt

1 In a food processor, pulse all the ingredients until you have a bright green paste, scraping down the sides of the processor if necessary.

2 Keep in a sealed jar in the fridge for up to 1 week.

Max's Go-to Salad Dressing

This works brilliantly with any salad, from simple lettuce leaves to leftover treasures such as beet, carrot, thinly sliced Brussels sprouts, mixed beans—all things salad. Perfect for in-a-pinch situations.

6 Tbsp extra-virgin olive oil
1 tsp Dijon mustard
1 tsp whole-grain mustard
1 Tbsp finely chopped fresh parsley
juice of ½ lemon
2 tsp maple syrup
¼ tsp black pepper

1　Put all the ingredients into a small jar, close the lid, and shake vigorously until smooth.

2　Keep in the fridge for up to 1 week.

Quick Garlic Chile Oil

Serve with nachos, or drizzle over pizza or noodle dishes such as Quick Garlic Chile Ramen (page 194).

⅓ cup vegetable oil
5 garlic cloves, finely chopped
3 tsp red pepper flakes
1 tsp sugar
½ tsp salt
1½ Tbsp apple cider vinegar

1　Put all the ingredients into a pan over medium heat and cook for 3–4 minutes, stirring often, until bubbles start to form; reduce the heat to low and cook until the garlic is fragrant. Leave to cool slightly before pouring into a jar.

2　When cool, add a thin layer of oil (about 1 tablespoon) on top of the sauce. Keep in the fridge for up to 2 weeks.

Coffee Cubes

Add to your iced coffee for an extra shot or, for the perfect morning smoothie, add 2–3 coffee cubes to a blender, add 1 ripe banana and a scoop of peanut butter, and top up with milk; blend until smooth.

1 Fill an ice cube tray with the last drops of coffee from your pot. Freeze overnight.

2 Keep in the freezer for up to 3 months.

Pickled Red Onion

The onion turns a bright pink shade and makes the perfect topping for curries, spiced lentils, burgers, or tacos.

½ red onion, thinly sliced
3 Tbsp white wine vinegar
1 Tbsp granulated sugar
pinch of salt

1 Put all the ingredients in a small bowl and gently mix; set aside for at least 15 minutes.

2 Keep in a sealed container in the fridge for up to 5 days.

Green Stock Cubes

Fun fact: you can freeze herbs! Preserve the intense flavors for months and easily add them into recipes.

large bunch of any leftover leafy green and/or fresh herb
1–2 garlic cloves and/or 1–2 Tbsp grated fresh ginger

1 Put your herbs and/or leafy greens in a large bowl and cover with boiling water for 30 seconds. Once they are bright green, drain the greens, then cover with cold water from the tap and leave for 1–2 minutes.

2 Drain the greens and/or herbs and place them in a blender or food processor. Add the garlic and/or ginger. Blend until you have a smooth green purée. You may need to add a little water to keep it smooth.

3 Pour the purée into an ice cube tray and freeze overnight.

Tip Use the green cubes in any dish from stir-fries and fried rice to soups and stews. Try them in my Easy Spinach and Chickpea Curry (page 159) and Creamy Leek and Parsnip Soup (page 22).

Hot Fudge Sauce

Pour this fudge sauce over brownies, cakes, cookies, and ice cream.

¼ cup full-fat coconut cream
2¼ oz dark chocolate, roughly chopped
½ tsp vanilla extract
2 Tbsp maple syrup
2 Tbsp unsweetened cocoa powder
½ tsp salt

1 In a small pan over low heat, combine the coconut cream, two-thirds of the chocolate, vanilla extract, and maple syrup. Stir until the chocolate melts, taking care not to burn the chocolate.

2 When the chocolate has melted, remove from the heat and whisk in the remaining chocolate, cocoa powder, and salt until no lumps or streaks of powder remain and the sauce is smooth. Serve warm.

Tip Keep any leftover hot fudge sauce in a sealed jar in the fridge for up to 2 weeks. Reheat in a small pan over low heat, stirring often, until warmed through.

Blueberry Compote

A great way to jazz up your morning porridge or toast, or serve with yogurt, ice cream, pancakes, waffles, muffins, scones—anything goes with this quick jam.

1⅓ cups fresh blueberries
zest of 1 lemon
2 tsp sugar

1 Put all the ingredients into a pan over medium-low heat. Crush some of the blueberries with the back of a spoon or fork, then simmer for 5–10 minutes over low heat.

2 Remove from the heat and let it stand for 5–10 minutes. The compote will thicken slightly as it cools.

3 To serve warm, reheat in a small pan over low heat, stirring occasionally, until warmed through.

4 Keep in a sealed container in the fridge for up to 7 days or freeze for up to 3 months.

Tips Swap blueberries for raspberries or strawberries.

Swap lemon zest for orange.

How to Get the Best Out of Your Food!

Storing food properly and avoiding waste can save you time and money.

	How to Store	How to Prep to Avoid Waste
Potatoes	• Cool, dark, dry, well-ventilated place, away from appliances that generate heat. • Don't refrigerate. • Keep separate from onions, garlic, bananas, and apples.	• Scrub; no need to peel. If you're a peeler, bake the skins to make chips. • If sprouting, remove sprouts; cut off small green bits, but if very green, compost.
Beets, carrots, parsnips, celeriac, rutabagas, turnips	• Remove green tops and store separately. • Refrigerate root veg in a reusable bag, in the bottom drawer.	• Scrub; no need to peel. • If soft, submerge in ice-cold water for 30 minutes to bring them back to life. • If the green tops are attached, remove them and wash to remove any dirt. Sauté the greens or make pesto.
Onions	• Cool, dark, dry, well-ventilated place, away from appliances that generate heat. • Don't refrigerate. Never store in plastic bags or airtight containers. • Keep separate from potatoes.	• Thinly slice off the top, but keep the root on. Cut in half from top to bottom. Peel the skin, then slice or chop down to the root. • Once chopped, refrigerate in a sealed container or wrapped in reusable plastic.
Garlic	• Store as for onions.	• To peel easily, place cloves of garlic in a jar, seal the lid, and shake vigorously for 5 seconds. The skin should fall off with a little help. • Use the entire clove, unless it's sprouting, in which case remove the green shoot.
Leeks, spring onions	• Refrigerate leeks in the bottom drawer. • Put spring onions in a jar with their roots in water; refrigerate, changing the water every other day.	• Don't throw away the green parts: they're edible. Thinly slice the green part and sauté. Slice the white part as close as you can to the root. Compost roots.
Tomatoes	• Room temperature, out of direct sunlight. • Store stem side down while they finish ripening. • Once ripe, use immediately, or keep in the fridge for a few days.	• Remove green stem, use everything else.

	How to Store	How to Prep to Avoid Waste
Eggplant	• Cool place, out of direct sunlight. Don't refrigerate. • Do not store in plastic. • Keep away from bananas, tomatoes, and melons.	• Remove green stem and compost. • Once sliced or chopped, instead of sprinkling salt to extract water/reduce bitterness, place the chopped eggplant in water and soak for 20 minutes. Take a handful of the eggplant and squeeze to remove excess water. The eggplant should be soft and ready to cook.
Peppers	• Refrigerate in the bottom drawer.	• Press the green stem until it breaks the skin, then remove. There's no need to remove the top third of the peppers. • Cut in half and remove seeds, then slice or chop. • Once cut, store in an airtight container in the fridge.
Zucchini	• Keep dry: don't wash until you're ready to use. • If not used within three days, store in a paper bag with one end open to encourage ventilation, for up to two weeks. Refrigerate in the bottom drawer. • Blanch and freeze.	• The entire zucchini is edible (including the flower). The stem is soft once cooked.
Winter squash (pumpkin, butternut, acorn, kabocha)	• These thick-skinned gourds can stay fresh and firm for months. Store in a cool, dry spot, out of direct sunlight. • Keep away from bananas, apples, and onions.	• Scrub; no need to peel. • Get as close as you can to the stem and root, slice them off, and compost. • Scoop out seeds, rinse in a bowl of water to remove pulp, pat dry, and bake the seeds. • Once cut, store flesh in an airtight container in the fridge.
Cucumber	• Refrigerate uncut in the bottom drawer for up to two weeks. • Wrap cut cucumbers tightly in reusable plastic.	• I never peel cucumbers, but if you do you can use the peel to infuse water, a fruity drink, or a cocktail. • Wash, then slice off the hard stem and compost.
Celery	• Refrigerate in the bottom drawer. • Submerge cut stalks in water in a sealed glass jar.	• Use the stalks and leaves. Slice off the bottom close to the root and compost.

How to Get the Best Out of Your Food!

	How to Store	How to Prep to Avoid Waste
Cabbage, broccoli, cauliflower	• Uncut heads can be refrigerated without a bag. • Once cut, store in an airtight container. • Blanch and freeze.	• Leaves, florets, cores, and stems are all good to eat. • If the outer part of the broccoli stem is tough, peel a little bit with a peeler or knife to get to the sweet, tender core; slice and cook as you would the florets. • Slice cabbage and cauliflower cores and cook with the florets. • Slice cauliflower leaves and add to a stir-fry or stew.
Leafy greens (kale, spinach, Swiss chard, salad leaves)	• Don't wash until you're ready to use: excess moisture encourages leafy greens to rot. • Refrigerate in the bottom drawer, in reusable ziplock bags. • Freeze and use in smoothies and sauces.	• Remove kale leaves from the stems; thinly slice or chop the stems. • With Swiss chard, the colorful stem is often delicate; chop or thinly slice the stems.
Herbs	• Rinse with water and dry thoroughly, then refrigerate in the bottom drawer. • Tender herbs (basil, chives, cilantro, dill, mint, parsley, etc): if you're using them within a day, no need to refrigerate, just snip off the bottom of the stems, remove any wilted or brown leaves, and place them in a jar or container with ⅛ inch of water. • Blend tender herbs with a little water and freeze in an ice cube tray.	• The stems of tender herbs offer subtle flavor to many dishes. Chop the stems and add at the start of any sauté; finely chop or purée to use in sauces.
Apples and pears	• Keep apples in the fruit bowl for up to a week; to store for longer, refrigerate in a paper bag in the bottom drawer. • Pears, if underripe, can be kept at room temperature; once soft, use immediately or stash them in the fridge for a day or two. • Squeeze a bit of citrus juice on exposed pieces of fruit to prevent them from browning too quickly. • Keep away from bananas.	• I never peel my apples, but if you do, you can use the peel to infuse water or fruity drinks. • Cut apple or pear in half and scoop out the seeds.

	How to Store	How to Prep to Avoid Waste
Mushrooms	• Store in the fridge in their original packaging or a paper bag for up to one week, but use as soon as possible.	• Use the entire mushroom, no need to peel the skin or remove the stems. Wipe off any dirt or give them a quick rinse, then use immediately.
Bananas	• Cool place, out of direct sunlight. Don't refrigerate. • Fully ripe bananas—if not eaten straightaway—should be peeled, sliced, and frozen in an airtight ziplock bag. • Squeeze a bit of citrus juice on exposed pieces of bananas, to prevent them from browning too quickly. • Keep separate from apples, avocados, and other fruits.	• If you dare, the skin is edible. Scrape away the fleshy bit on the inside of the skin, using a spoon. Thinly slice the skin and fry with onions and garlic in stews or curries or make my BLT (page 241).
Citrus fruits	• Store at cool room temperature for up to a week, or refrigerate to prolong their shelf life. • Refrigerate slices or half-cut fruit.	• Scrub the skins. • If waxed, you can soak them for a few minutes in a bowl of hot water and vinegar, then scrub to remove the wax coating. • If a recipe asks for zest and juice, zest the fruit first—it's a lot easier to zest when the fruit is whole. • To use the whole fruit, slice in half, remove the pips, then blend and freeze in ice cube trays (page 252).
Milk	• You can freeze milk. Pour into ice cube trays and use the frozen milk for smoothies, milkshakes, or in iced coffee.	• N/A
Yogurt	• Refrigerate on a lower shelf—not the fridge door. • Once opened, consume within 3–5 days. • Freezer friendly.	• N/A
Ginger	• Refrigerate in a reusable bag, in the bottom drawer.	• Wash if needed; no need to peel before grating or chopping.

How to Get the Best Out of Your Food!

	How to Store	**How to Prep to Avoid Waste**
Pasta	• Once opened, store dry, uncooked pasta in a cool, dry place for up to one year. Label and date, if necessary. I keep my pasta in an airtight container. • Fresh pasta: refrigerate and use by the use-by date. • Freeze unopened fresh pasta in its original packaging for up to six months.	• N/A
Bread	• Cool, dry area: a bread box is ideal. • Store in a paper bag, not plastic—plastic creates moisture and encourages mold. • Don't refrigerate and don't store on top of your fridge—this can speed up mold growth. • If you're not going to eat the bread within three days, slice and freeze—or freeze half the loaf as soon as you bring it home. • Process stale bread and freeze as breadcrumbs.	• N/A
Rice	• Store uncooked rice in a cool, dry place in an airtight container to keep out moisture. Use within 12–24 months. • To store cooked rice, spread it on a clean, lightly oiled baking sheet to cool evenly. Transfer the cooled rice to an airtight container or reusable bag; press the air out of the bag before sealing. • Reheat cooked rice over medium heat for 2–5 minutes (depending on quantity) until thoroughly hot. • To freeze cooked rice, cool and store in the same way. Use within six months.	• Add rice to a large bowl and wash with cold water. Drain the water, add fresh cold water and rinse again, repeating several times until the water is clear and not cloudy. This removes some of the starches and helps the rice cook more quickly.

Occasion Index

20 Minutes or Less

Best Festive Leftover Sandwich 244
Cheesy Garlic Bread 199
Chickpea "Tuna" Salad 129
Coffee Ground Pancakes 249
Extra Crunchy Onion Rings 189
Fresh Cucumber and Apple Salad 112
Garlic and Lemon Pangrattato 200
No-Bake Pumpkin Pie in a Jar 138
Quick Garlic Chile Ramen 194
Quick Gazpacho 95
Speedy Cherry Tomato Fettucine 86
Sticky Broccoli and Crispy Tofu 145
Sticky, Spicy Ginger and Garlic Tofu 126
Super Green Pancakes 170
Broccolini and Cream Cheese on Toast with
   Pickled Stems 196
Tomato, Feta, and Crushed Almond Salad 96

Brunch

Best Ever "Buttermilk" Pancakes 207
BLT 241
Carrot Lox and Bagel 16
Coffee Ground Pancakes 249
Salted Tomato Grilled Cheese 93
Sourdough French Toast with Glazed Peaches 80
Super Green Pancakes 170
Broccolini and Cream Cheese on Toast with
   Pickled Stems 196

Dinner Party

Baked Sun-Dried Tomato Rice with a Golden Pastry
   Lid 59–60
Baking Sheet Pesto Pizza 164–5
Blueberry Ginger Galette 226
Chocolate Orange Peanut Cheesecake 230
Cinnamon and Chocolate Churros 208
Citrus Cubes 252
Creamy Leek and Parsnip Soup with Parsnip Peel Chips 22
Crunchy Butter Rice, Cherries, and Toasted Hazelnuts 55–6
Fragrant Flatbreads 206
Greens and Feta Tarte Soleil 162
Mushroom Ravioli with Tofu Asparagus Purée 174–5
Salted Chocolate, Peanut Butter, and Tahini Brownies 219

Fan Favorites

Beet Bucatini 30
Best Ever "Buttermilk" Pancakes 207
Chickpea "Tuna" Salad 129
Crispy Smashed Potatoes with Spicy Lemon Mayo 36
Killer Tofu "Ground Beef" 128
Loaded Nachos and Carrot Cheese Sauce 19
One-Pan Lasagna 84
One-Tray Baked Gnocchi 89
Roasted Cauliflower That's Anything But Boring 154
Smoky Lentil and Broccoli Stem Tacos 142
Soft and Fluffy Potato Rolls 38
Spicy Baked Cauliflower Wings 148
Sticky, Spicy Ginger and Garlic Tofu 126
Tofu Butter "Chicken" 124
Triple Chocolate Birthday Cake 250

Festive

Buttery Herb Stuffing 74
Carrot Pecan Cake and Orange Drizzle 46
No-Bake Pumpkin Pie in a Jar 138
Nut Roast Cake with All the Trimmings 70–2
Roast Dinner Tart 119
Sticky Apple Toffee Pudding 233
The Best Roast Potatoes 33

For Sharing

Baking Sheet Pesto Pizza 164–5
Cheesy Garlic Bread 199
Extra Crunchy Onion Rings 189
Greens and Feta Tarte Soleil 162
Loaded Nachos and Carrot Cheese Sauce 19
Roasted Onion and Leek Dip 203
Roasted Root Veg Sub Sandwiches 66
Soft and Fluffy Potato Rolls 38
Spicy Baked Cauliflower Wings 148
Super "Meatball" Sliders 68

Pasta

Beet Bucatini 30
Brown Butter and Crispy Sage Mac and Peas 76
Caramelized Onion and Miso Mushroom Rigatoni 192
Cauliflower Ragù 146
Creamy Zucchini and Lemon Linguine 115
Fresh No-Egg Pasta 240
Fridge Greens Fusilli 160
Mushroom Ravioli with Tofu Asparagus Purée 174–5
One-Pan Lasagna 84
One-Pot Pantry Pasta 62
One-Tray Baked Gnocchi 89
Smoked Pea Carbonara 135
Speedy Cherry Tomato Fettucine 86
Stems and Herbs Pesto 156
Zesty and Herby Summer Orzo Salad 52

Summer Picnics or BBQ

BYOB (Build Your Own Bruschetta) 79
Fresh Cucumber and Apple Salad 112
Harissa Eggplant Kebabs with Zing Zing Grain Salad 97
Marinated Beets with Toasted Pistachios, Orange,
    and Mint 32
Mighty Green Quiche 158
Quick Gazpacho 95
Really Good Stuffed Peppers 100
Spicy Red Pepper Dip and Crispy Harissa Ground
    "Meat"102
Roasted Fennel and Quinoa Salad
    with Apple and Tahini 50
Sticky Eggplant and Peanut Salad 106
Tomato, Feta, and Crushed Almond Salad 96
Tomato Salad, Tofu Whip, and Garlicky Crumbs 90
Zesty and Herby Summer Orzo Salad 52

Sweet

Banoffee Moon Pies 236–7
Best Ever "Buttermilk" Pancakes 207
Blackberry Shortbread Frozen Yogurt 214
Blueberry Compote 268
Blueberry Ginger Galette 226
Carrot Pecan Cake and Orange Drizzle 46
Chocolate Orange Peanut Cheesecake 230
Cinnamon and Chocolate Churros 208
Citrus Cubes 252
Coffee Ground Pancakes 249
Fluffy Scones 217
Hot Fudge Sauce 268
Lemon and Poppy Seed Shortbread Fingers with
    Lemon Glaze 224
Lime Tart with Candied Lime Peel 255
No-Bake Pumpkin Pie in a Jar 138
No-Waste Cereal Milk Ice Cream 218
Passion Fruit and Mango Aquafaba Meringues 228
Salted Chocolate, Peanut Butter, and Tahini Brownies 219
Sourdough French Toast with Glazed Peaches 80
Spiced Apple Fritters 234
Spongy Banana and Chocolate Glazed Doughnuts 210–12
Sticky Apple Toffee Pudding 233
Strawberry Granita with Lemon Cream 229
Super Green Pancakes 170
Triple Chocolate Birthday Cake 250

Index

Note: Page references in *italics* indicate photographs.

A

Almond-Miso "Ricotta" and Grilled Zucchini Involtini, 121, *123*
Apple(s)
  Fresh, and Cucumber Salad, 112, *113*
  Fritters, Spiced, 234, *235*
  prepping and storing, 273
  and Tahini, Roasted Fennel and Quinoa Salad with, 50, *51*
  Toffee Pudding, Sticky, *232*, 233
Aquafaba
  Banoffee Moon Pies, 236–37
  Chickpea Mayo, 257, *258*
  Fresh No-Egg Pasta, 240
  Meringues, Passion Fruit and Mango, 228
  Triple Chocolate Birthday Cake, 250, *251*
Asparagus Tofu Purée, Mushroom Ravioli with, 174–75, *177*
Avocado and Tomato Salsa, 179

B

Bagel, Carrot Lox and, 16, *17*
Banana(s)
  Banoffee Moon Pies, 236–37
  BLT, 241, *242*
  and Chocolate Glazed Doughnuts, Spongy, 210–12, *211*
  prepping and storing, 274
  Super Green Pancakes, 170, *171*
Basil
  Carrot Top Pesto, 28
  Herby Lime Salsa, *258*, 263
  prepping and storing, 273
Bean(s). *See also* Chickpea(s)
  BYOB (Build Your Own Bruschetta), *78*, 79
  Loaded Nachos and Carrot Cheese Sauce, 19, *20*
  and Mushroom Casserole, Easy, *180*, 181
  and Peas Fritters, 132, *133*
  Rich Ribollita, 75
  Super "Meatball" Sliders, 68, *69*
Beet(s)
  Bucatini, 30, *31*
  and Carrots with Tahini Balsamic Vinaigrette, 26, *27*
  Marinated, with Toasted Pistachios, Orange, and Mint, 32
  prepping and storing, 271
  Roast Dinner Tart, *118*, 119
Berries
  Blackberry Shortbread Frozen Yogurt, 214, *215*
  Blueberry Compote, *258*, 268
  Blueberry Ginger Galette, 226, *227*
  Strawberry Granita with Lemon Cream, 229
Blackberry Shortbread Frozen Yogurt, 214, *215*

Black Pepper Tofu Stir-Fry, *104*, 105
Blueberry
  Compote, *258*, 268
  Ginger Galette, 226, *227*
Bread
  Broccolini and Cream Cheese on Toast with Pickled Stems, 196, *197*
  Buttery Herb Stuffing, 74
  BYOB (Build Your Own Bruschetta), *78*, 79
  Cheesy Garlic, *198*, 199
  Fragrant Flatbreads, 206
  Lentil Pappa Pomodoro, 136, *137*
  Rich Ribollita, 75
  Soft and Fluffy Potato Rolls, 38, *39*
  Sourdough French Toast with Glazed Peaches, 80, *81*
  storing, 275
Breadcrumbs
  Crispy Garlic, 30
  Garlic and Lemon Pangrattato, 200
Broccoli
  prepping and storing, 273
  Stem and Lentil Tacos, Smoky, 142, *143*
  Stem Fried Rice, 144
  Stems and Herbs Pesto, 156, *157*
  Sticky, and Crispy Tofu, 145
Broccolini and Cream Cheese on Toast with Pickled Stems, 196, *197*
Broth, Rich Garlic and Onion, 201
Brownies, Salted Chocolate, Peanut Butter, and Tahini, 219, *220*
Bruschetta, Build Your Own (BYOB), *78*, 79
Burger(s)
  Crispy Tofu, *130*, 131
  Leftover, Flatbreads, 248
  Meaty Mushroom, 188
  Super "Meatball" Sliders, 68, *69*

C

Cabbage
  Hispi Slaw, *34*, 35
  prepping and storing, 273
Cakes
  Carrot Pecan, and Orange Drizzle, 46, *47*
  Triple Chocolate Birthday, 250, *251*
Carrot(s)
  and Beets with Tahini Balsamic Vinaigrette, 26, *27*
  Cheese Sauce, Loaded Nachos and, 19, *20*
  Lox and Bagel, 16, *17*
  Nut Roast Cake with All the Trimmings, 70–72, *71*
  Pecan Cake and Orange Drizzle, 46, *47*
  and Potato Bake, Midweek, *24*, 25
  prepping and storing, 271
  Quick Pickled, 29
  Roast Dinner Tart, *118*, 119
  Top Pesto, 28
Cashews
  Creamy Zucchini and Lemon Linguine, 115
  Sour Cream, 19

Cauliflower
  Baked Sun-Dried Tomato Rice with a Golden Pastry
    Lid, *58, 59*–60
  prepping and storing, 273
  Ragù, 146, *147*
  Roasted, That's Anything But Boring, 154, *155*
  Wedges, Sticky, with Herby and Crunchy Rice, 152, *153*
  Wings, Spicy Baked, 148–49, *149*
Celeriac
  and Parsnip, Roasted, with Garlicky Grains and Creamy
    Tahini Sauce, 18
  prepping and storing, 271
Celery, prepping and storing, 272
Cereal Milk Ice Cream, No-Waste, 218
Chard, prepping and storing, 273
Cheese. *See also* Cream Cheese
  Baking Sheet Pesto Pizza, 164–65, *166*
  Brown Butter and Crispy Sage Mac and Peas, 76, *77*
  Cheesy Garlic Bread, *198*, 199
  Greens and Feta Tarte Soleil, 162, *163*
  One-Pan Lasagna, 84, *85*
  Salted Tomato Grilled, *92*, 93
  Tomato, Feta, and Crushed Almond Salad, 96
Cheesecake, Chocolate Orange Peanut, 230, *231*
Cherries, Crunchy Butter Rice, and Toasted Hazelnuts,
    54, 55–56
Chickpea(s)
  Curried Couscous with Sticky Butternut and Cilantro
    Chutney, *64,* 65
  Mayo, 257, *258*
  and Pumpkin, Curried, 120
  Roasted, 257
  and Spinach Curry, Easy, 159
  "Tuna" Salad, 129
Chile
  Garlic Oil, Quick, *259,* 265
  Garlic Ramen, Quick, 194, *195*
Chocolate
  Banoffee Moon Pies, 236–37
  and Cinnamon Churros, 208, *209*
  Glazed and Spongy Banana Doughnuts, 210–12, *211*
  Hot Fudge Sauce, 268, *269*
  Orange Peanut Cheesecake, 230, *231*
  Peanut Butter, and Tahini Brownies, Salted, 219, *220*
  Triple, Birthday Cake, 250, *251*
Churros, Cinnamon and Chocolate, 208, *209*
Chutney, Cilantro, *64, 65*
Cilantro
  Chutney, *64, 65*
  Herby Lime Salsa, *258,* 263
  prepping and storing, 273
Cinnamon and Chocolate Churros, 208, *209*
Citrus. *See also specific citrus fruits*
  Cubes, 252, *253*
  prepping and storing, 274
Coconut cream
  Chocolate Orange Peanut Cheesecake, 230, *231*
  No-Bake Pumpkin Pie in a Jar, 138, *139*
Coffee Ground Pancakes, 249

Composting, 9
Compote, Blueberry, *258,* 268
Corn
  "What's in the Fridge?" Fried Rice, 57
Couscous
  Curried, with Sticky Butternut and Cilantro Chutney,
    64, 65
  Really Good Stuffed Peppers, 100, *101*
Cream Cheese
  and Broccolini on Toast with Pickled Stems, 196, *197*
  Carrot Lox and Bagel, 16, *17*
  Chocolate Orange Peanut Cheesecake, 230, *231*
Cucumber(s)
  Fresh, and Apple Salad, 112, *113*
  Leftover Burger Flatbreads, 248
  prepping and storing, 272
  Salsa, Crisp, 114
  Zesty and Herby Summer Orzo Salad, 52, *53*
Curried Couscous with Sticky Butternut and Cilantro
    Chutney, *64,* 65
Curried Pumpkin and Chickpeas, 120
Curry, Easy Spinach and Chickpea, 159

D

Dates
  No-Bake Pumpkin Pie in a Jar, 138, *139*
  Sticky Apple Toffee Pudding, *232, 233*
Dips
  Roasted Onion and Leek, 203
  Spicy Red Pepper, with Crispy Harissa Ground "Meat,"
    102, *103*
Doughnuts, Spongy Banana and Chocolate Glazed,
    210–12, *211*

E

Eggplant
  Charred, and Peanut Stew, *98,* 99
  Harissa, Kebabs with Zing Zing Grain Salad, 97
  prepping and storing, 272
  Ratatouille Grain Bowl, 109
  and Squash, Roasted, with Tahini Yogurt and Toasted
    Seeds, 116, *117*
  Sticky, and Peanut Salad, 106, *107*
Everything Seasoning, *262,* 263

F

Fennel, Roasted, and Quinoa Salad with Apple and
    Tahini, 50, *51*
Flatbreads
  Fragrant, 206
  Leftover Burger, 248
Food labeling, 12
Food storage, 10–11, 271–75
Freezer storage, 11
French Toast, Sourdough, with Glazed Peaches, 80, *81*
Fridge storage, 11

Fritters
  Peas and Beans, 132, *133*
  Spiced Apple, 234, *235*
Frozen Yogurt, Blackberry Shortbread, 214, *215*
Fruits. *See also specific fruits*
  cleaning, 12

G

Galette, Blueberry Ginger, 226, *227*
Garlic
  Bread, Cheesy, *198,* 199
  Chile Oil, Quick, *259,* 265
  Chile Ramen, Quick, 194, *195*
  and Lemon Pangrattato, 200
  and Onion Broth, Rich, 201
  prepping and storing, 271
Gazpacho, Quick, *94,* 95
Ginger
  Blueberry Galette, 226, *227*
  and Garlic Tofu, Sticky, Spicy, 126, *127*
  prepping and storing, 274
  Quick Garlic Chile Ramen, 194, *195*
Gnocchi, One-Tray Baked, *88,* 89
Grain(s). *See also specific grains*
  Garlicky, and Creamy Tahini Sauce, Roasted Parsnip
    and Celeriac with, 18
  Ratatouille Bowl, 109
  Salad, Zing Zing, Harissa Eggplant Kebabs
    with, 97
Granita, Strawberry, with Lemon Cream, 229
Greens. *See also specific greens*
  and Feta Tarte Soleil, 162, *163*
  Fridge, Fusilli, 160, *161*
  Green Stock Cubes, 267
  leafy, prepping and storing, 273
  One-Tray Baked Gnocchi, *88,* 89

H

Harissa
  Eggplant Kebabs with Zing Zing Grain Salad, 97
  Ground "Meat," Crispy, Spicy Red Pepper Dip with,
    102, *103*
Hazelnuts, Toasted, Crunchy Butter Rice, and Cherries,
  54, 55–56
Herb(s). *See also* Basil; Cilantro
  DGS (Delicious Green Sauce), *258,* 261
  Green Sauce, 66, *67*
  Green Stock Cubes, 267
  -Lemon Mayonnaise, 241
  prepping and storing, 273
  Roasted Root Veg Sub Sandwiches, 66, *67*
  and Stems Pesto, 156, *157*
Hot Fudge Sauce, 268, *269*

I

Ice Cream, No-Waste Cereal Milk, 218

Ice cubes
  Citrus Cubes, 252, *253*
  Coffee Cubes, *266,* 267
  Green Stock Cubes, 267

K

Kale
  Crispy, Udon Noodles and Peanut Butter Miso
    Dressing, 168
  Mighty Green Quiche, 158
  Pesto, 164, *166*
  prepping and storing, 273
Kitchen guidelines, 9–13

L

Lasagna, One-Pan, 84, *85*
Leek(s)
  and Onion, Roasted, Dip, 203
  and Parsnip Soup, Creamy, with Parsnip Peel Chips, 22, *23*
  prepping and storing, 271
Leftovers, 12
Lemon
  Citrus Cubes, 252, *253*
  Cream, Strawberry Granita with, 229
  and Garlic Pangrattato, 200
  -Herb Mayonnaise, 241
  and Poppy Seed Shortbread Fingers with Lemon
    Glaze, 224, *225*
  prepping and storing, 274
Lentil(s)
  and Broccoli Stem Tacos, Smoky, 142, *143*
  Nut Roast Cake with All the Trimmings, 70–72, *71*
  One-Pan Lasagna, 84, *85*
  One-Pot Pantry Pasta, 62, *63*
  Pappa Pomodoro, 136, *137*
Lime
  Citrus Cubes, 252, *253*
  prepping and storing, 274
  Salsa, Herby, *258,* 263
  Tart with Candied Lime Peel, 255

M

Mango and Passion Fruit Aquafaba Meringues, 228
Maple Miso Mustard, 241
Mayonnaise
  Chickpea Mayo, 257, *258*
  Lemon-Herb, 241
"Meat," Ground
  Crispy Harissa, Spicy Red Pepper Dip with, 102, *103*
  Meaty Mushroom Burgers, 188
  Super "Meatball" Sliders, 68, *69*
Meringues, Passion Fruit and Mango Aquafaba, 228
Milk, storing, 274
Miso
  -Almond "Ricotta" and Grilled Zucchini Involtini, 121, *123*
  Maple Mustard, 241

Mushroom and Caramelized Onion Rigatoni, 192, *193*
Peanut Butter Dressing, Crispy Kale Udon Noodles
    and, 168
Moon Pies, Banoffee, 236–37
Mushroom(s)
    and Bean Casserole, Easy, *180,* 181
    Broccoli Stem Fried Rice, 144
    Burgers, Meaty, 188
    Crispy, Risotto, 178
    and "Egg" Noodles, Takeout-Style, 186, *187*
    Leftover Stuffing Stuffed, 246, *247*
    Masala and Crispy Cardamom Rice, 182, *183*
    Miso, and Caramelized Onion Rigatoni, 192, *193*
    Pad Thai, 184, *185*
    prepping and storing, 274
    Pulled, Tacos with Avocado and Tomato Salsa, 179
    Ravioli with Tofu Asparagus Purée, 174–75, *177*
    Super "Meatball" Sliders, 68, *69*
Mustard
    Maple Miso, 241
    Tahini Lemon Sauce, 154

N

Nachos, Loaded, and Carrot Cheese Sauce, 19, *20*
Nectarines
    Quick Gazpacho, *94,* 95
Noodles
    Mushroom Pad Thai, 184, *185*
    Quick Garlic Chile Ramen, 194, *195*
    Sticky, Spicy Ginger and Garlic Tofu, 126, *127*
    Udon, Crispy Kale, and Peanut Butter Miso Dressing, 168
Nut(s). *See also specific nuts*
    Kale Pesto, 164, *166*
    Roast Cake with All the Trimmings, 70–72, *71*

O

Oil, Quick Garlic Chile, *259,* 265
Onion(s)
    Caramelized, and Miso Mushroom Rigatoni, 192, *193*
    and Garlic Broth, Rich, 201
    and Leek, Roasted, Dip, 203
    Pickled Red, *259,* 267
    prepping and storing, 271
    Rings, Extra Crunchy, 189, *190*
Orange(s)
    Chocolate Peanut Cheesecake, 230, *231*
    prepping and storing, 274
    Toasted Pistachios, and Mint, Marinated Beets with, 32

P

Pad Thai, Mushroom, 184, *185*
Pancakes
    Best Ever "Buttermilk," 207
    Coffee Ground, 249
    Potato, Spiced, 42–43, *43*
    Super Green, 170, *171*

Parsnip(s)
    and Celeriac, Roasted, with Garlicky Grains and
        Creamy Tahini Sauce, 18
    and Leek Soup, Creamy, with Parsnip Peel Chips, *22, 23*
    prepping and storing, 271
    Roast Dinner Tart, *118,* 119
Passion Fruit and Mango Aquafaba Meringues, 228
Pasta
    Beet Bucatini, 30, *31*
    Brown Butter and Crispy Sage Mac and Peas, 76, *77*
    Caramelized Onion and Miso Mushroom Rigatoni, 192,
        193
    Cauliflower Ragù, 146, *147*
    Creamy Zucchini and Lemon Linguine, 115
    Fresh No-Egg, 240
    Fridge Greens Fusilli, 160, *161*
    Mushroom Ravioli with Tofu Asparagus Purée, 174–75,
        177
    One-Pan Lasagna, 84, *85*
    One-Pot Pantry, 62, *63*
    One-Tray Baked Gnocchi, *88,* 89
    Smoked Pea Carbonara, *134,* 135
    Speedy Cherry Tomato Fettuccine, 86
    Stems and Herbs Pesto, 156, *157*
    storing, 275
    Takeout Style Mushrooms and "Egg" Noodles, 186, *187*
    Zesty and Herby Summer Orzo Salad, 52, *53*
Peaches, Glazed, Sourdough French Toast with, 80, *81*
Peanut Butter
    Banoffee Moon Pies, 236–37
    Charred Eggplant and Peanut Stew, *98,* 99
    Chocolate, and Tahini Brownies, Salted, 219, *220*
    Miso Dressing, Crispy Kale Udon Noodles and, 168
    Peanut Sauce, *258,* 261
    Sticky Eggplant and Peanut Salad, 106, *107*
    "What's in the Fridge?" Fried Rice, 57
    Zesty Tahini, Roasted Sweet Potatoes with, 44, *45*
Peanut(s)
    Chocolate Orange Cheesecake, 230, *231*
    Mushroom Pad Thai, 184, *185*
    and Sticky Eggplant Salad, 106, *107*
    Takeout Style Mushrooms and "Egg" Noodles, 186, *187*
Pears, prepping and storing, 273
Pea(s)
    and Beans Fritters, 132, *133*
    Carbonara, Smoked, *134,* 135
    Mac and, Brown Butter and Crispy Sage, 76, *77*
    Zesty and Herby Summer Orzo Salad, 52, *53*
Pecan(s)
    Carrot Cake and Orange Drizzle, 46, *47*
    No-Bake Pumpkin Pie in a Jar, 138, *139*
Pepper(s). *See also* Chile
    Black Pepper Tofu Stir-Fry, *104,* 105
    prepping and storing, 272
    Ratatouille Grain Bowl, 109
    Romesco Risotto, 108
    Spicy Red, Dip with Crispy Harissa Ground "Meat,"
        102, *103*
    Stuffed, Really Good, 100, *101*

Pesto
  Carrot Top, 28
  Kale, 164–65, *166*
  Stems and Herbs, 156, *157*
Pickled Red Onion, *259,* 267
Pizza, Baking Sheet Pesto, 164–65, *166*
Poppy Seed(s)
  Everything Seasoning, *262,* 263
  and Lemon Shortbread Fingers with Lemon Glaze,
    224, *225*
Potato(es). *See also* Sweet Potato(es)
  and Carrot Bake, Midweek, *24,* 25
  Crispy Smashed, with Spicy Lemon Mayo, 36, *37*
  Pancakes, Spiced, 42–43, *43*
  prepping and storing, 271
  Roast Dinner Tart, *118,* 119
  Roasted, The Best, 33
  Rolls, Soft and Fluffy, 38, *39*
  and Spring Onion Cakes, *34,* 35
Pudding, Sticky Apple Toffee, *232,* 233
Pumpkin
  and Chickpeas, Curried, 120
  Pie in a Jar, No-Bake, 138, *139*
  prepping and storing, 272

Q

Quiche, Mighty Green, 158
Quinoa and Roasted Fennel Salad with Apple and Tahini,
  50, *51*

R

Ratatouille Grain Bowl, 109
Rice
  Baked Sun-Dried Tomato, with a Golden Pastry Lid, *58,*
    59–60
  Broccoli Stem Fried, 144
  Crispy Cardamom, and Mushroom Masala, 182, *183*
  Crispy Mushroom Risotto, 178
  Crunchy Butter, Cherries, and Toasted Hazelnuts, *54,*
    55–56
  Herby, Golden Split Peas with, 61
  Herby and Crunchy, Sticky Cauliflower Wedges with,
    152, *153*
  rinsing and storing, 275
  Romesco Risotto, 108
  "What's in the Fridge?" Fried, 57
Rolls, Soft and Fluffy Potato, 38, *39*
Romesco Risotto, 108

S

Salad Dressing, Max's Go-to, *264,* 265
Salads
  Carrots and Beets with Tahini Balsamic Vinaigrette,
    26, *27*
  Chickpea "Tuna," 129
  Fresh Cucumber and Apple, 112, *113*

Grain, Zing Zing, Harissa Eggplant Kebabs with, 97
greens for, prepping and storing, 273
Marinated Beets with Toasted Pistachios, Orange, and
  Mint, 32
Orzo, Zesty and Herby Summer, 52, *53*
Roasted Fennel and Quinoa, with Apple and Tahini, 50, *51*
Roasted Squash and Eggplant with Tahini Yogurt and
  Toasted Seeds, 116, *117*
Sticky Eggplant and Peanut, 106, *107*
Tomato, Feta, and Crushed Almond, 96
Tomato, Tofu Whip, and Garlicky Crumbs, 90, *91*
Salsa
  Avocado and Tomato, 179
  Crisp Cucumber, 114
  Herby Lime, *258,* 263
Sandwiches
  Best Festive Leftover, 244, *245*
  BLT, 241, *242*
  Roasted Root Veg Sub, 66, *67*
  Salted Tomato Grilled Cheese, *92,* 93
Sauces
  Delicious Green (DGS), *258,* 261
  Green, 66, *67*
  Hot Fudge, 268, *269*
  Peanut, *258,* 261
  Tahini Mustard Lemon, 154
  Tomato, Simplest, 87
Sausages, plant-based
  One-Tray Baked Gnocchi, *88,* 89
Scones, Fluffy, *216,* 217
Seasoning, Everything, *262,* 263
Seeds
  Everything Seasoning, *262,* 263
  Kale Pesto, 164–65, *166*
  Lemon and Poppy Seed Shortbread Fingers with
    Lemon Glaze, 224, *225*
  Toasted, and Tahini Yogurt, Roasted Squash and
    Eggplant with, 116, *117*
Shortbread Fingers, Lemon and Poppy Seed, with
  Lemon Glaze, 224, *225*
Slaw, Hispi, *34,* 35
Sliders, Super "Meatball," 68, *69*
Soups
  Creamy Leek and Parsnip, with Parsnip Peel Chips, 22, *23*
  Lentil Pappa Pomodoro, 136, *137*
  Quick Gazpacho, *94,* 95
  Rich Ribollita, 75
Spinach
  and Chickpea Curry, Easy, 159
  Mighty Green Quiche, 158
  prepping and storing, 273
  Super Green Pancakes, 170, *171*
Split Peas, Golden, with Herby Rice, 61
Spring Onion(s)
  and Potato Cakes, *34,* 35
  prepping and storing, 271
Squash. *See also* Pumpkin; Zucchini
  Curried Couscous with Sticky Butternut and Cilantro
    Chutney, *64,* 65

and Eggplant, Roasted, with Tahini Yogurt and Toasted Seeds, 116, *117*
Roast Dinner Tart, *118,* 119
winter, prepping and storing, 272
Stew, Charred Eggplant and Peanut, *98,* 99
Sticky Apple Toffee Pudding, *232,* 233
Stock, Veg Scraps, *258,* 260
Stock Cubes, Green, 267
Strawberry Granita with Lemon Cream, 229
Stuffing
Best Festive Leftover Sandwich, 244, *245*
Buttery Herb, 74
Leftover, Stuffed Mushrooms, 246, *247*
Roast Dinner Tart, *118,* 119
Sweet Potatoes
Nut Roast Cake with All the Trimmings, 70–72, *71*
Roasted, with Creamy and Zesty Tahini Peanut Butter, 44, *45*

T

Tacos
Lentil and Broccoli Stem, Smoky, 142, *143*
Pulled Mushroom, with Avocado and Tomato Salsa, 179
Tahini
and Apple, Roasted Fennel and Quinoa Salad with, 50, *51*
Balsamic Vinaigrette, Carrots and Beets with, 26, *27*
Chocolate, and Peanut Butter Brownies, Salted, 219, *220*
Mustard Lemon Sauce, 154
Peanut Butter, Zesty, Roasted Sweet Potatoes with, 44, *45*
Sauce, Creamy and Garlicky Grains, Roasted Parsnip and Celeriac with, 18
Yogurt and Toasted Seeds, Roasted Squash and Eggplant with, 116, *117*
Tarts
Greens and Feta Tarte Soleil, 162, *163*
Lime, with Candied Lime Peel, 255
Roast Dinner, *118,* 119
Tofu
Asparagus Purée, Mushroom Ravioli with, 174–75, *177*
Black Pepper Stir-Fry, *104,* 105
Butter "Chicken," 124, *125*
Crispy, and Sticky Broccoli, 145
Crispy, Burgers, *130,* 131
"Ground Beef," Killer, 128
Lime Tart with Candied Lime Peel, 255
Loaded Nachos and Carrot Cheese Sauce, 19, *20*
Mighty Green Quiche, 158
Smoked Pea Carbonara, *134,* 135
Sticky, Spicy Ginger and Garlic, 126, *127*
Whip, Tomato Salad, and Garlicky Crumbs, 90, *91*
Tomato(es)
and Avocado Salsa, 179
Baking Sheet Pesto Pizza, 164–65, *166*
BLT, 241, *242*
BYOB (Build Your Own Bruschetta), *78,* 79
Cauliflower Ragù, 146, *147*
Cherry, Fettuccine, Speedy, 86
Feta, and Crushed Almond Salad, 96
Grilled Zucchini and Miso-Almond "Ricotta" Involtini, 121, *123*
Lentil Pappa Pomodoro, 136, *137*
One-Pan Lasagna, 84, *85*
One-Pot Pantry Pasta, 62, *63*
One-Tray Baked Gnocchi, *88,* 89
prepping and storing, 271
Quick Gazpacho, *94,* 95
Rich Ribollita, 75
Salad, Tofu Whip, and Garlicky Crumbs, 90, *91*
Salted, Grilled Cheese, *92,* 93
Sauce, Simplest, 87
Sun-Dried, Rice with a Golden Pastry Lid, Baked, *58,* 59–60
Turnips, prepping and storing, 271

V

Vegetables. *See also specific vegetables*
Best Festive Leftover Sandwich, 244, *245*
cleaning, 12
Rich Ribollita, 75
Roasted Root, Sub Sandwiches, 66, *67*
Veg Scraps Stock, *258, 260*

W

Walnuts
One-Pan Lasagna, 84, *85*
Romesco Risotto, 108
Spicy Red Pepper Dip with Crispy Harissa Ground "Meat," 102, *103*

Y

Yogurt
Frozen, Blackberry Shortbread, 214, *215*
Marinated Beets with Toasted Pistachios, Orange, and Mint, 32
Minty, 25
storing, 274
Tahini, and Toasted Seeds, Roasted Squash and Eggplant with, 116, *117*

Z

Zucchini
Grilled, and Miso-Almond "Ricotta" Involtini, 121, *123*
and Lemon Linguine, Creamy, 115
prepping and storing, 272

Notes

Acknowledgments

A lot of incredible women are behind this book.

Thank you to my literary agent Rachel Mills, who was a big supporter of my work way before we even started working together. It almost feels as though fate brought us together! I absolutely love working with you and feel so grateful for your honesty and dedication, and for always finding the time for me.

Thank you to Lizzy Gray. You are a powerhouse.

Thank you, Sam Crisp, Alice King, and the entire Ebury team who had their heads, hands, eyes, and tastebuds involved in the making of this book. Thank you for steering *You Can Cook This!* in the best possible direction.

Lizzie Mayson, you are a ray of sunshine. Thank you for capturing the essence of my food and ethos in every single photo. Your photography is out of this world and I can't wait to continue working with you.

Thank you, Elena and Esther, for your help developing these recipes and for styling them so beautifully. Without you and your brilliant team, this book wouldn't be anywhere near as delicious. The recipes are foolproof and so are YOU!

Thank you to my online community. Without your support this book simply wouldn't exist. I don't want to get too gushy, but you really have changed my life and I will never take it for granted.

Lastly, I'd like to thank my wife, Venetia—my sous chef, personal food critic, and love. Thank you for challenging me to think in new ways and for guiding me in the best possible way. I'll always be here to cook you whatever you want. You truly are my favorite person to eat with and nothing feels more like home to me than you (and a bowl of pasta).

Published in the United States by Rodale Books, an imprint
of Random House, a division of Penguin Random House LLC,
New York.

Originally published in the United Kingdom in 2023 by Ebury
Press, an imprint of Ebury Publishing. Ebury Press is part of
the Penguin Random House group of companies.

RODALE and the Plant colophon are registered trademarks of
Penguin Random House LLC.

rodalebooks.com
randomhousebooks.com

Library of Congress Control Number: 2022948382

ISBN 978-0-593-57872-8
Ebook ISBN 978-0-593-57873-5

Printed in China

Book design by Evi-O.Studio | Evi O. & Emi Chiba
Cover photograph by Lizzie Mayson

10 9 8 7 6 5 4 3 2 1

First US Edition